Advance Praise for Just One Step

"I decided long ago that I would read, study and listen to whatever Jeff Nischwitz shares with the world. I have personally seen and experienced his gift in helping others navigate life. *Just One Step* will not only transform your life, but the lives of those you love and lead."

—**Tommy Spaulding,** *New York Times* Bestselling author of *The Heart-Led Leader* and *It's Not Just Who You Know*

"Sometimes in life it's enough to 'Just Be Present' and sometimes we have to 'Just Walk Backwards' in our journey, seeing where we've been to better know where we're going. *Just One Step* takes us through a journey in which Jeff does an amazing job of challenging us both to be present *and* to press full steam ahead, thinking differently in every aspect of our lives. This book speaks volumes to the multitude of people who sometimes get stuck in the routine of life. Thank GOD for a man like Jeff Nischwitz that's courageous enough to provide his friends and readers with 'arrows of truth' that inspire us to think bigger, dream larger, and execute intentionally on life's amazing journey every day!"

—**M. Scott Diggs,** Entrepreneur & CEO

"One of the most exciting things about this inspiring and deeply spiritual book is the remarkably vivid experience that each page serves up, an expansion of mind and spirit as we're taken on a truly profound journey alongside one of the most talented and gifted writers I know. Jeff is able to express his personal journey in a way that is deeply relatable, authentic, and raw. I was in tears before I even began the journey with Jeff's heartfelt letter to his mother, and as I continued on with Jeff's pilgrimage, somehow I too was personally transforming. Thank you, Jeff, for gifting us a magical experience, full of grace, lessons, and love. 'Every journey begins and continues with just one step' will be my new mantra!"

—**Nichole Lowe,** CEO & Founder, Sole Life

"I LOVE THIS BOOK! In *Just One Step*, Jeff shares in a raw and vulnerable way from the opening pages about his precious mother to the closing chapter where he gives the reader a practical road map to navigate life. I especially find Chapter 11 riveting, in which Jeff dives deeper into how your WHY can help you overcome life's biggest obstacles and even become unstoppable. This is not your average book because Jeff is not your average person. When you dive into these pages, you will have a better view of the you that you really want to be!"

—**Justin Jones-Fosu,** Social Entrepreneur, Speaker
and Author of *Your WHY Matters NOW*

"*Just one Step* explores the journey of Jeff Nischwitz, a journey of living, loving and letting go. *Just One Step* is inspirational and motivating, as Jeff puts to print what he eats, sleeps and breathes. His experiences personally and professionally bring insights that most coaches lack. Working with Jeff over the years has helped me grow not only professionally, but personally as well. Jeff challenges you to dig deep, look at the big picture and allow yourself to be vulnerable — vulnerable to the truth, past and present. *Just One Step* hits home on so many levels and allows us to see that through our choices in life, we end up where we are meant to be. Jeff, thank you for the window into your journey — looking forward to the next adventure!"

—**Betsy Sterling,** Executive Vice President, Beaver Excavation

"In *Just One Step*, Jeff invites the reader to join him on his transformational El Camino journey, an experience that taught and/or affirmed for him a wealth of life lessons in just a few short weeks. *Just One Step* is replete with tales of Jeff's encounters on the trail, perspectives he gained, and truths that were validated. Jeff skillfully translates his learnings on the trail to day-to-day living, challenging the reader to think and act differently and providing an actionable guide to apply these learnings in your own life. The only question is, after reading *Just One Step*, will the Camino call you as well?"

—**David J. Akers,** President & CEO of Sourcing Alliance

"Jeff Nischwitz is definitely someone who 'walks the talk.' The vulnerability and integrity he calls for from others are on full display to all who know him. In *Just One Step*, Nischwitz 'talks the walk' as readers are guided along the Camino de Santiago in Spain and through daily life as well. The book provides analogies and simple lessons with immediate application in all aspects of life. Readers' questions and struggles are anticipated and responded to in this profoundly impactful 'walking conversation' with the author."

—**Maureen Beck,** Teacher, Coach, Principal and School Leader

"Since I first met Jeff, I have seen him grow in many ways - confidence, spiritual connection, service, goodness, and peace. I think his journey to a peaceful 'I'm good no matter what' perspective allows him to enter any situation with grace and be the rock that others need in a storm. Jeff's journey on the Camino was certainly one of those big shifts for him. I felt a palpable change in his demeanor when he returned from the Camino, and I knew the journey had changed him forever. This story is one for each of us as we attempt to challenge ourselves to find our greatness, or even to get through the next day. Jeff has shared his deep heart and keen mind with us in this book, and I highly recommend reading, absorbing, and living this book with him."

—**Craig Mathews,** Chief Thinkologist, Big Think Innovation

"For me, one of Jeff Nischwitz's greatest gifts is being real. Saying what he experiences how he experiences it. I love this about him personally, and I appreciate how he models this very necessary practice for all of us in his books. *Just One Step* is no different. They often say we can begin with the end, and in that spirit, I love the last words that Jeff wrote in his journal on his Camino journey, the journey that is so much of this book: '*The Camino is not a life altering experience – it's a life accessing experience.*' We can all use the stories of Jeff's adventures to assess our own life journey, now and wherever we may roam."

—**Traci Philips,** Executive Identity & Performance Coach,
The Innate Coach

"There are many who write and speak about different and better ways to live and lead, but rarely do the messengers live and lead in full alignment with their message. Jeff Nischwitz is the exception. In *Just One Step,* Jeff shares not only the stories of his Camino de Santiago journey, but the lessons he brought home which he lives out every day. Different ways to live, lead, relate and impact ... one simple step at a time."

—**Dr. Kevin Snyder,** Professional Speaker and
Author of *Think Differently to Achieve Success*

"Jeff Nischwitz again immediately pulls us into his book and has us curious about the connections he makes with others on his Camino journey with 'vulnerability and intimacy,' as he so aptly puts it. Jeff draws out great analogies between embracing our journey in life and walking the Camino, including the symbolism of the stones Jeff found along the way, his truths behind them, and how what we carry can keep us from fully living our life experiences. If you're searching for healing, breakthrough or even transformation, *Just One Step* provides insight and inspiration, as well as a great read!"

—**Judy Harrelson,** President, Orare, Inc.: Healthy Homes,
Healthy Families, Healthy Environment

"Jeff is a man who has dedicated his life to exploring the deeper truth within himself, and he relates those experiences in what I would call 'lessons learned for life' in *Just One Step.* I was moved, touched and inspired by his thoughts on living an authentic, purposeful and meaningful life. A must read for anyone interested in transformational living and personal development."

—**Dennis F. Shackley,** Full Leader, The Mankind Project

"*Just One Step* takes you on a journey of the Camino trail in a way that feels like you're a 'voyeur in a backpack,' listening in on the author's thoughts and experiencing his highs and lows. It doesn't matter if you've never had the inclination to do a long hike, it's about the journey in Jeff's book. As someone who has experienced her own trail, hiking across the Grand Canyon rim to rim to rim, I can attest to the ups and downs and the change that can occur with just one step."

—**Marcey Rader,** Founder, Work Well, Play More!

"Jeff is an engaging storyteller, partly because of the fantastic adventures he has gone on, but more importantly because of the depth of reflection he has wrestled with. Through the pages of this book you will encounter the story that Jeff is living and not simply be entertained but also stretched and inspired to craft an even greater story with the life you have been given. The principles and concepts within the pages of this book will add enormous value to you in whatever role or situation you find yourself in. Do yourself a favor and invest your time into reading and applying what Jeff shares in *Just One Step*."

—**Jonathan A. Buckland,** Pastor & Spiritual Leader,
The Bridge Church

"Once again, Jeff provides valuable insight and gold nuggets to help us maneuver on our own yellow brick road journey in life, both personally and professionally. Jeff's invitation and guidance on just letting go is something that I have come to regularly practice. I notice trying to force something usually takes away from it happening. When I surrender, let the flow of things happen naturally and do not worry about the outcome, I find I am usually very happy with how things turn out; if it's not originally how I thought it would be, it's not meant to be, and I more often than not learn something important along the way."

—**Jennifer Cabic,** Naturopath, Wholistic Integration, LLC

"*Just One Step* is a journey of awakening, discovery, and awareness. The simple-to-follow ideas in the book are brought to life through the stories of Jeff's amazing journey on the Camino de Santiago. Jeff provides a useful 5 x 4 *Life Formula* to navigate your life forward, one step at a time. Each chapter also contains a little ultreia (you'll learn about it in the book). I encourage you to read this book, then leverage it to create an additional dose of energy in your life."

—**Stan Phelps,** Founder of StanPhelpsSpeaks.com and
author of the *Purple Goldfish* Series of Books.

Just One Step

Blessings on
your own personal
journey of
Just One Step!

Jeff

Just One Step

Walking Backwards to the Present on the Camino Trail

jeff nischwitz

EAGLE HEART
PRESS

Tampa, Florida

Published by Eagle Heart Press
12312 Adair Court
Tampa, FL 33626
www.eagleheartpress.com

ISBN: 978-0-9984097-1-9 (softcover)
ISBN: 978-0-9984097-2-6 (ebook)
ISBN: 978-0-9984097-3-3 (hardcover)
ISBN: 978-0-9984097-4-0 (audiobook)
Library of Congress Control Number: 2020903360

Printed in the United States of America

Editor: Ben Barnhart
Cover Design: Mike Steele, vitalink (www.vitalinkweb.com)
Layout Design: Katherine Lloyd, The DESK (www.thedeskonline.com)
Interior Journal Photograph: Thom Sivo Photography
Back Cover Photograph: Michael T. Lowe Photography

The Camino is not a life altering experience –
it's a life accessing experience.

—Jeff Nischwitz, Final Camino Journey Entry

Contents

Gratitude

*I*t was Mother's Day 2018 – just a few months after my Mom had passed away – and I was sitting in church feeling a wide range of emotions. With all the focus on mothers in the service, most of my feelings were sadness. I had also been feeling a great deal of frustration with myself over the prior couple of weeks. I had been thinking about writing what has become this book since shortly after returning from Spain in June of 2017, but thinking about it certainly isn't doing it. Despite my strong feelings that it was important to write a book about my journey and, more important, who I have become through and since that journey, I had neither committed to it nor started it. I had also become aware that there must be some fear or resistance related to writing this book, which certainly showed itself once I started writing.

Because of all of these feelings – fear, uncertainty and frustration – in April I had made a personal commitment that I would make a final decision about writing this book by May 15, 2018. There was no rhyme or reason for picking that date other than it being approximately 30 days later. As of May 13, 2018 (Mother's Day), I had not yet made a decision, and my deadline was two days away. As I sat in church that Sunday morning, I asked God for clarity about the book – am I meant to write this book or not – and the answer came that morning.

While sitting in church on Mother's Day, and without even thinking about the book, the dedication came to me in clear and precise words, and in that moment I knew the answer was yes, and I made the commitment to share all of this with the world and each of you. These are the words that came to me like a lightning bolt that Sunday morning:

Thank you Mom! Thank you for loving me. Thank you for all the excitement you shared with me and others about my travel adventures, including the Camino. I know you were worried about me and that you worry about me when I travel, but you never shared those worries with me. Instead, you asked questions, expressed excitement with each of my stories, and rooted me on with the simplest **question:** *Where are you off to next? Most important, thank you Mom for believing in me even when it wasn't easy and even when I was off course in my life. I know you'll be with me on all the journeys for the rest of my life wherever they take me. This book is for you, Mom!*

As with all books, there are always so many people to thank. I'm extremely grateful for my friend Mark LeBlanc, who coached and mentored me on this Camino experience. I'm grateful for all my friends who encouraged me as I prepared for the Camino. I'm grateful for the many people I met and experienced on my Camino journey in Spain, many of whom you'll learn more about in this book. I'm grateful for Martin Sheen and Emelio Estevez for the heart and soul they put into the movie *The Way*, which launched my journey to the Camino de Santiago. I've read or listened to their interviews about the movie, and it's clear to me that neither of them saw *The Way* as just a movie. Their intentions for and in *The Way* are certainly what reached out, grabbed me and compelled me towards the Camino.

I'm deeply grateful for the Mankind Project International (www.mkp.org) and the many men who have been part of my healing journey through and with this organization. My life's journey, my Camino experience and the transformational work that I've been a part of wouldn't have occurred without my initial exposure to the Mankind Project and my ongoing involvement with and mentorship from the organization.

Last and never least, I'm grateful for the people who played a role in making this book a reality. As always, I'm so grateful to my long-time editor Ben Barnhart, who once again worked his magic on this book. Thank you for not only making my writing and this book better, but for understanding and preserving my voice, challenging me with your questions and encouraging me with your ongoing comments and input regarding the ways that my words and messages resonate with and impact you. Thank you also to my layout partner for this book, Katherine Lloyd. From our very first phone conversation, I knew that you were the right person to work with on *Just One Step*. Thank you for seeing this book and me as more than just another book project, and for truly connecting to the journey and its messages. Thank you, Ben and Katherine, for making this book all that it is with words and, most important, heart, soul and spirit.

Finally, thank you to my fellow Master Mind 500 members, who pushed me, challenged me, encouraged me and loved me through the process of bringing *Just One Step* to life. Thank you Marcey Rader, Stan Phelps, Justin Jones-Fosu, Kevin Snyder and David Rendall. I'm grateful that we've all come together to help each other spread our words, messages, inspiration and impact farther, faster and deeper.

And now, let's begin our journey to the Camino de Santiago together with the very first step of many—and always with gratitude!

Foreword

by Mark LeBlanc, CSP

*I*n your hands, you hold a book that will have a profound impact in how you think, feel and act in your life. No matter where you are on your path – you will find wisdom and principles that will guide and shape the next chapter of your life and work.

I first met Jeff by chance, or shall I write, by divine appointment. Little did I know at the time, we would have more than one, hand-of-God appointments. I've found him to be curious, thoughtful, sensitive and intense. It was an honor to walk the walk with Jeff, listen to him talk the walk and now read about his experiences.

You'll meet Jeff for the first time or get to know him better as he describes his extraordinary journey along the Way of Saint James. You would do well to keep his book handy and refer to it often on your journey. It will be a lighthouse guide in directing your decisions and inspiring your actions along the way. It will be a catalyst in helping you become as successful and fulfilled as you choose to become.

I hope you have an opportunity to meet Jeff, hear him speak and even hire him to walk alongside you on the Camino of your life. You will be glad you did.

If you're ready for different outcomes in your leadership and life, *Just One Step* and its many lessons will serve you well on your journey. One thing is certain -- you and your life will *never be the same* – only better for it.

Buen Camino!

—**Mark LeBlanc, Certified Speaking Professional**
Speaker, Philanthropist, Pilgrim and Author of
Never Be the Same and *Growing Your Business!*

Chapter 1

The Calling

*I*t was April 3, 2015, and I was wrapping up a long week of business in Raleigh, NC. I was staying at a LaQuinta Inn, and when I went to bed on Friday night, I was excited at the prospect of sleeping in. I didn't have to be up at any particular time, I was exhausted, and I was looking forward to the rare sleep-in opportunity. And then I woke up at 3:00 AM, without knowing that this early morning awakening would shift the trajectory of my life.

That morning I was persistent, and I tried for three hours to get back to sleep, continually getting more frustrated that I was missing out on the sleeping in experience. Finally, I gave up at 6:03 a.m. – I remember it because I looked at the clock and decided to turn on the television. When I turned it on, a movie was starting on that opening channel, and I decided to watch it even though I hadn't even seen the title. Two hours later, when the movie was over, I knew that my life had been forever changed.

The movie was *The Way* (2011), starring Martin Sheen and directed by his son, Emilio Estevez, which tells the story of a father (Martin Sheen) who travels to France to retrieve the body of his son, who died while walking the Camino de Santiago. The father then decides to take the Camino journey himself in the hope of understanding his son, but he ends up having his own learning and healing experience. I had never heard of the Camino or *The Way* before, but numerous times during the movie I broke into weeping tears. By the third time I knew, and I said out loud, "I have to do this journey." At the time, I didn't know why – I was just listening to something inside me – and even when I left for my Camino journey I still didn't know why. I just knew that I'd been called and I was listening.

Thus began a two-year journey that led to me being on the Camino de Santiago in May of 2017, having already been blessed in many ways and through many synchronicities even before I arrived in Spain for my Camino experience. If I've learned one thing over the past two years in sharing my stories about the Camino, it's that not everyone knows about the Camino. Having discovered and now experienced the Camino myself, it's easy for me to assume that you all know about it. For that reason, it's important to share just a little bit now with you (at the beginning) so you can sit back and enjoy the journey through this book.

El Camino de Santiago is Spanish for "The Way of Saint James," and represents a pilgrimage journey to the Cathedral of Santiago de Compostela in Santiago, Spain. There are actually three different Caminos that are traveled today. The first is the Camino Frances (or French Camino), which is the most famous and heavily traveled and covers approximately 500 miles. This is the Camino that I walked in 2015. Second is the Camino Norte (or Northern Camino), which covers approximately 512 miles. Third is the shorter Camino Portugues (or Portugal Camino), which covers approximately 383 miles. All three Caminos officially end in Santiago in northern Spain.

The Camino (as all three are collectively known) has existed as a Christian pilgrimage for well over a thousand years and likely existed earlier as a pre-Christian route. The Camino became known as the Way of Saint James based upon the legend that the remains of Jesus's apostle Saint James the Elder are interred in the Cathedral in Santiago. In early times, the Camino was largely a religious pilgrimage for its travelers, but over thousands of years it has evolved into a pilgrimage that draws travelers for many different reasons. Some still walk the Camino for religious reasons and experiences. Others walk the Camino for spiritual reasons.

The Calling

Some walk the Camino simply for a journey of solitude. Others walk the Camino to get away from life or to find answers. Others walk the Camino because they've had something significant happen in their life (e.g. job loss or change, death, relationship ending, etc.) and want or need to get away. Some walk the Camino for the physical exercise, and some walk it simply for the achievement (because it's there). Of all the people I met and spoke to on the Camino, every one of them had one or more reasons to be on the Camino and nearly all of them were on some sort of personal quest.

Just as there are many reasons that pilgrims walk the Camino, there are many ways to experience the Camino. What every pilgrim seems to have in common is that they were in some way called or compelled to the Camino, and that each person viewed the Camino as a journey and an experience – not just a random thing they were doing. Certainly, my calling to the Camino and my experience of the journey were both profound and magical. Even more important than the experience, though, is what I learned and who I became because of my Camino journey, all of which I gift to you through the words, stories, messages and lessons that follow. It's now time to begin our journey together through this book, a journey that begins with magic and the knowledge that every journey always begins and continues with Just One Step.

Chapter 2

Camino Magic

*A*s I limped into the Spanish city of Santiago de Compostela (and the limping was very real), I had only two thoughts in mind – get to the Cathedral (the "official" end of the Camino) and find somewhere to get off my feet and lie down. I'd pushed myself hard that day, covering 24.25 miles on bad shins and bad feet. I'd begun my Camino journey six days earlier and had covered an aggressive 125 miles (20-plus miles per day) despite several physical setbacks. And yet, I was thrilled to be arriving in Santiago and already looking forward to my further walking journey to the sea (the cities of Fisterra and Muxia on the Atlantic Ocean). While my journey wasn't yet complete, I was now an official Camino pilgrim, having arrived in Santiago.

After my journey toward walking the Camino de Santiago began with the movie *The Way*, I was encouraged and supported in making my own Camino pilgrimage by my friend and mentor Mark LeBlanc, who was also in Spain on his third full Camino journey in 2017. Mark had shared on Facebook that he would enter Santiago the same day as me, albeit three hours ahead of me. Mark had also indicated that he planned to stay in an albergue (a hostel only for Camino pilgrims) about three miles outside of Santiago. When I arrived in Santiago, I assumed that Mark had completed his Camino journey and was now resting comfortably outside of the city.

I headed to the Camino office in Santiago to receive my certificate and to be included in the official registry, and despite the fact that the office was supposed to close at 9:00 PM, it was already closed at 8:05 PM (apparently, they close the office when the line inside is sufficient to take them until 9:00 PM). I was disappointed, but I could come back the next day, so I was back to my second priority – finding a place to rest and lie down. I'd already had several occasions on the Camino where there was no place to stay (I'd chosen not to make reservations because this was an adventure, after all), but Santiago is a city of 100,000 people with hundreds of places to stay (albergues, hostels, hotels, etc.).

I walked up the street from the certification office and walked into the first albergue I found, but the answer to my inquiry for a bed was "completo" (no beds). I walked into a second albergue and the answer was the same – completo. While I knew I'd find a place to stay, I was beyond exhausted and my feet and shins were killing me. I just wanted somewhere to lie down.

Just up the block I saw a small sign marked "Hotel." I walked towards it telling myself that I'd stay there if they had a room, even if the cost was higher than an albergue. It was a very small hotel, and I later learned that it only had twelve rooms. The lobby area was appropriately small for a twelve-room hotel, and when I inquired, I heard these glorious words: "We have one room." I took it and began the check-in process, which included Camino Passport, U.S. Passport, credit card, etc.

As I was digging through my backpack for items, I periodically lifted my head to answer the clerk's questions, all the time relishing the idea that I'd soon be getting a hot shower and lying down. I was literally light-headed and barely able to stand. As I looked up to answer yet another question, I saw someone standing in front of me in the lobby and, wondering if it was a mirage, I said (almost to myself), "Mark?" I shook my head, looked again and repeated, "Mark?" Finally, aware that the person standing in front of me was in fact my good friend, Mark LeBlanc, I exclaimed, "Mark!" As I teared up at the sight of my friend and gave him a giant hug, I asked him, "What are you doing here?" Mark replied, "I'm staying in this hotel." At this I added, "Guess this means we're having dinner."

You see, Mark had checked into an albergue outside the city (where he has stayed before), but then he decided to check out and come back into Santiago, choosing to stay at the very same hotel that I'd stumbled into. Remember, Santiago is a city of 100,000 people with hundreds of places to stay, and both Mark and I had "randomly" picked the same hotel. In addition, Mark shared with me that the only reason he was walking out of the hotel at that very moment was to find a cell phone store because his phone wasn't working (which means we couldn't even have communicated with each other). If he hadn't walked out of his room at that very time, we'd have missed each other and never known we were staying in the same twelve-room hotel.

Most of you may be thinking coincidence, but some of you are thinking perfect synchronicity (aka Camino magic), and this book is a guide for those of you who believe in synchronicity or are at least open to its possibilities. My Camino magic moment with Mark in Santiago was near the end of my journey, but throughout my Camino journey I experienced profound lessons, meaningful insights and life lessons that have transformed my personal, professional and leadership journey through life.

If you're thinking you have to walk the Camino to have these same experiences, you do not. You can have the experiences anywhere because what's most important isn't the Camino journey but embracing the lessons and shifts that I brought back from my Camino journey, which I'm sharing in this book. My journey allowed me to bring the Camino into my life, and my deepest desire is that this book and your experience of it will allow you to bring the Camino into your life as well.

This book is a guide for those of you who believe in synchronicity or are at least open to its possibilities.

I knew I needed to write this book because the shifts that I've experienced since my Camino journey have created a life experience with virtually no stress, with more peace and joy, with a profound sense of groundedness, in a deep state of presence, and a resulting experience of feeling and being virtually invincible and unstoppable. Yes, I still get shaken by life, but I'm now able to consciously and swiftly recover and get back to the present. I want to share this journey, these lessons and these shifts with each of you so that you can experience the same levels of peace, joy and empowerment in every part of your life and leadership. I want you to be unstoppable. Now, let's begin your journey to unstoppable together with … *Just One Step.*

Chapter 3

Just the Facts

*M*y physical journey to Spain and the Camino de Santiago began on May 23, 2017, when I flew to Madrid, Spain. I flew back to the United States on June 7, 2017, after my sixteen-day adventure. I spent the first couple of days exploring Madrid, and from there I flew to Santiago de Compostela (the official ending of the Camino), where I boarded a bus to take me back up the Camino to begin my journey.

I started my Camino journey in the city of Villafranca del Bierzo, which I chose because I wanted to get in as many miles as possible on the Camino with the time I had available. I spent a long time looking at cities up the Camino from Santiago on the map. I settled on Villafranca del Bierzo because I believed that I could make the journey to Santiago and then on to the sea before I had to leave Spain. I knew from the beginning that I had to go past Santiago and on to the sea because I've always been drawn to water, especially the ocean.

There are two coastal cities (Fisterra and Muxia) that you can walk to after you arrive in Santiago, and the journey to both cities on the sea will add approximately 80 miles to your Camino journey. What they call the full Camino de Santiago, from Saint-Jean-Pied-de-Port, France to Santiago is 800 kilometers (approximately 500 miles), and including the two cities on the sea makes the entire Camino Frances journey approximately 580 miles.

From my starting point in Villafranca del Bierzo to Santiago and then on to the sea, I journeyed 200 miles on the Camino, and I was on the Camino for eleven days (ten days of walking). That's an average of twenty miles every day of just walking. On the Camino your day consists of walking. You get up, you walk, you eat lunch, you walk, you find a place to sleep (albergues, hostels, hotels, etc.), you eat dinner, you sleep, and you get up the next morning and do it all again. That's the Camino reality, but every day is filled with a wide range of sights, people and experiences.

For some of you these distances will sound significant, and for others they may lack context. I was planning to walk around 200 miles when I left for Spain, but it didn't hit me how far that was until I realized that the distance from my home in Cleveland to Dayton, OH (my hometown) is 205 miles. I realized that I was planning to walk from Cleveland to Dayton! For my Raleigh friends, Boone, NC is 193 miles from Raleigh. For my St. Louis friends, Springfield, MO is 194 miles away. For my Denver friends, Steamboat Springs is 195 miles from Denver. For my Tampa friends, Jacksonville is 199 miles from Tampa. For my San Diego friends, Santa Barbara is 215 miles from San Diego. Take a moment and figure out what city or town is 200 miles from where you live and let that sink in. For those of you who are step counters, my Camino journey was approximately 380,000 steps.

My first day on the Camino was quite interesting. After having an unexpected, unplanned and synchronistic dinner with my Camino mentor (Mark Leblanc) in Villafranca del Bierzo, I had a challenging day (on the second most difficult leg of the Camino, I'm told) – sun, rain, extensive elevation climbs and exhaustion. Rather than stopping in one village with someone that I'd walked with at the end of the day, I decided to walk on another 1.5 miles to the next town. That's when I got my first true taste of how quickly things can change on the Camino.

My God moment came in the form of a prayer that went like this: "You've got this, right?"

I was walking along the top of a ridge and was halfway to the next town when the light rain suddenly turned into a storm. Within moments, the rain was coming down in sheets, and despite my poncho I was soaked to the bone. Then, in an instant, the temperature dropped twenty degrees, the rain turned to stinging hail and the lightning storm began. Here I was, walking along the top of a ridge in the middle of a hail, rain, wind and lightning storm (picture the golf course storm scene in the movie *Caddyshack*), and with two metal poles in my hands. And I don't do well with electricity or lightning, not since my younger brother Gregg was electrocuted in a painting accident in 1980. I was scared – real fear – and I didn't have much of a choice since either direction (back or forward) was the same distance and there was no shelter in sight. I was feeling truly alone, and that's when I had my first true moment with God on the Camino.

My God moment came in the form of a prayer that went like this: "You've got this, right?" Immediately, I felt a palpable relief come over me – a calm and peace that "surpasses all understanding" (Philippians 4:7 NKJV). Upon feeling this sense of calm and protection I thought to myself, "That was so cool and real." God was indeed walking with me on this Camino journey.

When I arrived in the next town (O Cebreiro), I got my first taste of another Camino experience – no room at the inn. I had chosen not to make any reservations for a place to stay on the Camino. While you can make reservations at albergues, hostels and hotels (in larger cities), I wanted the adventure of not knowing where or when I'd stop each day. It was part of the adventure, and it resulted in situations where I didn't have a place to stay (this and two other times), and each time I was required to walk a long distance to find a place to lay down my head, while I was experiencing great pain in both of my feet (see below). My first "no room at the inn" experience came in O Cebreiro, as I limped into town cold, wet and hungry and discovered that there were no more places to sleep that night. For reasons that I didn't understand at that moment, I wasn't worried, troubled or concerned in any way. I knew I'd be okay – I'm always okay – and we're all always okay.

I found my way into a chaotic bar which was packed with fellow Camino pilgrims, many soaked to the bone like me, and I could feel the frenetic energy in the room as people were scrambling to find a place to stay. After talking to one person, I was told to talk to David, a tall young man who clearly stood out in the crowd – he was American, could speak Spanish and was working with a nearby hotel that had rooms available and would pick us up and bring us back to O Cebreiro in the morning to continue our journey. I talked to David, and soon I had a room booked at the nearby hotel (nearby in terms of driving – it was 10 miles away), where a soft bed and warm shower awaited me. I later learned that David was walking the Camino with his father, Andy. They'd started in France (the beginning of the Camino Frances) and had been on the Camino for over twenty days.

I had dinner that night with David, his father and the other Camino pilgrims who had come to the hotel, and I sat next to David. During dinner, David asked me about the bar back in O Cebreiro. He said that when I approached him at the bar he was certain that I already had a place to sleep that night (which I did not). When I asked him why, David said that he'd noticed me in the bar (I'm big and tall too and stand out in a crowded room) – specifically, he noticed how calm I was. Most of the people in the bar were frantic and nervous, but he said that I looked like I didn't have a worry in the world. That's why he was surprised to learn that I didn't already have a place to lay my head that night. And David was right – I wasn't worried or concerned in any way. I knew that somehow or some way I'd be okay and that this was all part of the Camino adventure and the adventure of life. I have now also come to embrace this reality as part of my daily living – that I and things will be, and in fact already are, okay.

I had already scouted out dry doorways and a church where perhaps they would let me sleep on the floor. No matter what happened, I knew that the worst that would happen is that I'd have a difficult night of sleep, or even no sleep, but I'd be okay. This was day one on the Camino, and I'd brought this peace, calm and surrender (I don't control things outside of myself) with me, but I had no idea that I'd discover an even deeper and more profound sense of peace, calm, presence and surrender on the Camino – a discovery that I've brought back from the Camino, integrated into my life and which I'll share with you throughout this book.

The most important other facts for you to know about my journey relate to my feet and ankles, since they form the foundation for much of this journey and framed my Camino experience. Certainly, blisters are a common occurrence on the Camino, even if you've trained well and have the right boots, and I had my share of blisters: five big ones that didn't heal until after my journey. More significant, however, were the two shin splints that I encountered: my left shin on day two and my right shin on day three. Thankfully, I'd brought along an ankle brace that I was able to use on my left shin until I found a town with a pharmacy on day four where I could buy some tape for both shin splints. If you know about shin splints you know two things – they're very painful, and the best treatment is rest (not twenty miles of walking every day on various surfaces and terrains).

Even more significant were the painful problems that developed on the balls of both my feet starting on day three. Since returning, we've determined that the issue relates to my feet (not my boots), and I've been advised that the use of a small pad will fix the issue. However, these painful spots on both my feet meant that every step – every step – I took on the Camino starting on day three came with a pain level of anywhere from four to eight. The typical pain level was four to six, but when I stumbled on a rock and didn't land just right, the pain was an eight and it literally brought me to my knees and tears to my eyes. This was the painful reality of my Camino journey, along with the swelling that came with it.

From the third day on, at night I'd take off my boots and literally limp somewhere for dinner. My limp was so bad that many people couldn't believe that I was still walking the Camino. One person I met on the Camino (Roger) told me one night that he thought he was going to have to carry me across the street to my albergue. While I iced my shins every night and was pounding the Ibuprofen every day, the relief was minimal, and every night I said a prayer that my feet wouldn't hurt so bad the next day. Every morning before I got down off the bunk bed to the floor, I again prayed that the pain would be less than the day before. It never was, which I realized each morning when my feet painfully hit the floor. And each day I'd bandage my blisters and the painful spots on my feet, tape my shins, put on my wool socks, and lace up my boots to begin another day on the Camino. These are the facts of my Camino journey which form the foundation of all that I'm about to share with you and the many lessons I learned that I now gift to you.

Chapter 4

Just Who

Along the road
Your steps may stumble
Your thoughts may start to stray
But through it all a heart held humble
Levels and lights your way.
Excerpt From "Along The Road" By Dan Fogelberg

M y journey on the Camino de Santiago was one of solitude, aloneness and quiet contemplation. It was also a journey of connection,
albeit often brief and for only moments, and my Camino experience was
filled with and blessed by the many people I met along the road. While
they're not always part of the lessons and experiences of the Camino,
their stories and my connection with them are all pieces of my Camino
experience, and they all enriched and enlivened my travels – so much so
that I feel compelled to share many of them with you. My hope is that
you too will experience them and their stories (in some cases our shared
stories) in ways that will enrich your experience of this book and, more
important, enrich your life's journey.

Empathy and Purpose

On my second day on the Camino, I walked alone much of the morning (which was common). I also felt a strong need to be alone with the

grief of learning via text of my Uncle Chuck's death that morning. Late in the morning, however, I found myself walking past a tall, thin man who looked about my age. He also looked very fit! I said hello and discovered that he spoke English, and we began a conversation. Alex (all names are changed in this book) was from the Netherlands, and when I asked him where he'd started his journey, he said "Holland." Thinking he thought I was asking where he was from, I clarified my question and he repeated, "Holland." I learned that Alex had *walked from Holland* to the Camino (approximately 700 miles), only to begin the 500-mile Camino journey. Incredible, I thought as he shared the story of his walk from Holland and through France just to *begin* the Camino.

I also learned that this was Alex's second Camino journey. His first Camino was three years earlier and was, in his words, "for healing" as he was struggling in his life. Alex and his wife started and now operate an organization that helps children and teens with autism learn how to live independently, and it had grown so large that Alex was no longer doing what he loved. They'd scaled back the business, and his current Camino trip was more for enjoyment and connection.

Eventually, Alex shared with me that after his last Camino journey he'd learned that he has a form of autism himself, which explained why he'd always understood the people that he served. We talked about walking in someone's shoes, and it turned out that Alex was "walking in their shoes" since he too had a form of autism, which is why he has always had such great empathy for them and a deep desire to help them. This doesn't mean that we can only serve those like us or that empathy requires a shared experience, but my walk and talk with Alex reminded me of two things: the gift of empathy and the power of purpose. Alex and his wife have created a business founded upon a heartfelt purpose and mission of service. As I wrote in my journal that evening about my time with Alex, "This was my first gift of the day!"

My walk and talk with Alex reminded me of two things: the gift of empathy and the power of purpose.

Vulnerability and Compassion

I met so many people along the Camino road, some for brief moments and some for extended conversations, but the next person I want to share with you was only for a brief conversation. It was my third morning on the Camino, and I had stopped in the town of Samos (famous for the beautiful Monastery of St. Julian of Samos, which dates from at least the 8th Century). I was leaving late that morning but decided to stop and get a quick and simple breakfast of a scone and orange juice (a typical Camino breakfast). I was sitting outside the little café with my already aching shin splints elevated and iced, and I was the only person there. Soon a man sat down a few tables away from me, and we began to chat (also common on the Camino).

Dennis was an Anglican priest from Toronto, and he'd taken a four-month sabbatical, which included his three-month walk on the Camino. He shared a little bit about his family (his wife and 19-year old twin daughters) and that today was his birthday. He then shared with me an experience he had early during his Camino experience. He'd been walking several days and was missing his wife and daughters, and he also was still grieving the recent death of this father. He was sitting on a bench weeping, when a woman walked by and asked him if he wanted space or if she could sit with him. Dennis had met this woman before on the Camino, and didn't particularly like her, but he invited her to sit with him. Soon she was literally holding him as he wept. This woman was just what Dennis needed that day and in that moment, and what he needed came from this totally unexpected source.

As Dennis shared his experience with me, it struck me that the Camino is about vulnerability (Dennis sharing his story with me, a total stranger, and his willingness to openly grieve) and about compassion (this stranger, a woman he didn't even like, who would sit and hold him as he openly wept). Dennis went on to share that the Camino is a great place to grieve and how he'd already had many intimate conversations on his Camino journey. I was gifted with Dennis and his story early on my Camino journey, and it helped to form my experience. In my journal for this day I wrote the following comment: "Maybe that's why I'm here on the Camino – intimacy and vulnerability." Dennis was my gift that day – a gift that I still carry in my heart. I'm always reminded of the way that this woman (a virtual stranger) didn't try to comfort Dennis, but merely created space and allowed him to be sad while she held him (and his sadness) on the Camino.

Grief and Healing

As you'll read later in this book, the Camino carried a strong grief message for me, and I was confronted with grief along the way, starting on my second day when I learned of my Uncle Chuck's death. I wrote this in my journal on the morning that I learned that Uncle Chuck had died: "I'm sad that I didn't know Chuck more or better." Grief stalked me on the Camino, including in a conversation on my third day when I met Henry from Germany. Henry was sitting on a log when I passed him, and he asked if he could walk with me (Camino travelers are very respectful and always ask if you're open to them walking with you). Within just a few minutes, he shared several intimate stories, including some of his therapy experiences.

Henry also shared with me that his mother had died when he'd been on the Camino only one week. Wow, I thought, his mother passed and he decided to stay on the Camino. It began to make more sense as Henry shared with me that he'd also had many issues with his mother over his lifetime. As Henry put it, "She did not do well as a mother when I was young." Henry told me that he decided to stay on the Camino when his mother died because he'd already "made peace with her" before his journey and that he'd "healed his relationship" with her. It was powerful to hear Henry share about the challenges in his life and in his relationship with his mother, and of his decision to continue his Camino journey when she died. My initial response was one of surprise, but I now understand it. While I don't know what my decision would have been, I can easily see how staying on the Camino made perfect sense for Henry.

I learned something about grief and healing (and intimacy) from Henry, and I'm so grateful that he asked to walk with me and that we shared a few hours together along the road on the Camino.

Connection and Letting Go

On day five, I wore my *Hamilton* t-shirt (from the Broadway hit), the only cotton shirt I took on my journey because cotton is not the best material for hiking. I walked alone all morning until someone told me that they liked my t-shirt. This was the beginning of my time with Tom from Virginia. Tom had recently retired, and his wife had passed away nine years earlier. Grief had once again shown up on my Camino journey.

Tom and I walked and talked for about three hours and then shared lunch together, and our conversations were deep, vulnerable and intimate. We shared about grief and loss, about relationships (past and present), about being parents and the challenges when our children are struggling. I loved the connection I experienced with Tom, and it was the only time on my Camino journey where phone numbers were exchanged.

Apparently, my time with Tom also opened me up to my own deeper questions about many things, and my journal notes show a great deal of reflection that afternoon (after I parted ways with Tom), especially about relationships. I was pondering my current romantic relationship – what it was and what it wasn't, as well as how I was showing up in it. I also wrote down a simple yet profound **question:** "Am I really ready to commit? Really?" I thought so, but it turns out in hindsight that I wasn't ready. Still more healing to be done. It was also during my walk with Tom that I realized that I still needed to let go of a past relationship. It was long over, but it still had a hold on me in some hard-to-understand way. I stopped next to a stream to take a break, and I wrote this in my journal:

I could feel the release of whatever it was I was still hanging on to, and in that moment I knew that I had finally let go and that it was time to move on in my life.

> "Goodbye!
> I may always love you, and I believe you love me,
> but it won't happen and I'm letting you go."

It was a simple ritual and just a few words, but it had a profound impact on me. I could feel the release of whatever it was I was still hanging on to, and in that moment I knew that I had finally let go and that it was time to move on in my life. This door somehow was opened through my conversation with Tom, which was an incredible gift.

Unmasking and Synchronicity

My most fascinating Camino interaction came on day nine. After walking alone all morning, a woman from Germany, Adele, started talking with me. In that moment I didn't really want to talk to anyone, but she seemed to want company. We only walked and talked for about an hour, but it was a memorable hour. Adele told me that she'd come the Camino to get answers, but that so far she'd mostly uncovered more questions. I chuckled at this and told her that I wasn't surprised – when I go looking for answers I often get more questions, but better questions. I suggested that she be patient and let the answers come to her, rather than seeking them out.

When I asked Adele what she did, she shared with me that she's a professional clown, and her clown name is Abiala. I had never met a clown before, and I had so many questions, including this one: Who's the most true you – Adele or Abiala? For some reason, her answer didn't surprise **me**: "Abiala is the most real. Adele wears masks."

After sharing this, Adele asked me if I knew what she meant by wearing masks, at which point I laughed out loud. I then explained to Adele that I was also an author and that I had written a book about taking off masks (*Unmask: Letting Go of Who You're "Supposed" to Be & Unleashing Your True Leader*). When I then showed Adele a picture of the cover of my book, she was astonished, and I realized that this was the reason that I had met her that day.

Like so many things on the Camino and in life, everything happens for a reason, including the people who show up. The question is not whether synchronicity is real, but whether you're open to it so that you can see and experience it as it unfolds. It's all around us and all around you, but you'll miss it if you deny it or close your mind and heart to it.

You may not always understand it or know the reason for it (perhaps not for many years), but synchronicity is real if you listen for it, just like I listened to the small voice that told me to walk and talk with Adele.

I saw Adele a couple of other times on the Camino, including on my last day in the town of Fisterra. I was sitting on a porch having breakfast when she walked up to me. Despite all the miles and the passage of time, our paths had crossed this one more time at the end of the Camino. Adele had loved her connection with the Camino and talked about possibly moving there. She also told me that she certainly would be back to the Camino again, and she has honored that commitment. I'm so grateful that Adele unmasked herself with me and shared some of her innermost thoughts and feelings. Adele was an amazing gift to me and a reminder that the world is filled with people who are wearing masks and looking for answers, whether it's on the Camino or walking by me (and you) every day.

Joy for Living

Of the many people I met on the Camino, whether for long talks or brief moments of conversation, the most memorable person is Roger. I never walked with Roger, but our paths kept crossing (once again, the magic of synchronicity). Roger sat down at my table on the sidewalk the evening of my fourth day. This is common on the Camino – having someone sit down at your table to share space, but not necessarily conversing. I loved that there was no expectation that you had to engage with someone, and you could sit together without feeling the need to fill the space.

Roger and I sat next to each other journaling for about an hour as I sipped my red wine and Roger drank his beer, and when we both had finished writing we began to chat. I learned that this was Roger's third full Camino walk and that he took the journey about every two years. Roger said he likely wasn't coming back because the Camino had gotten too crowded and there was too much talking and too many casual walkers on the Camino. We shared dinner and several drinks together that night, and Roger let me know that he really enjoyed his beer (but "never during the day" and never more than three ... which I later learned was not true).

Roger had a unique perspective on the Camino. Unlike so many people who got up before the sun and started walking in the dark, Roger's goal was to be the last one to leave every morning. When I asked what he would do if I was still hanging around in the morning, he said he'd wait for me to leave. We actually ended up seeing each other in the morning over juice and a scone, and indeed he was the last one to leave.

I didn't expect to see Roger again, but the next night I saw him walking across the street in a fairly large town and headed to the restaurant where I was having dinner. He was staying in the same albergue as me, and we had yet another dinner together. This time Roger was talking about how many people are emotional on the Camino, which was confusing to him. When I asked him if he'd experienced any emotion on the Camino, Roger said, "Yes, I cried when my favorite football team lost." That's Roger. He also showed me a picture of his wife and daughters, and when I commented that his wife was very beautiful, he said, "Only on the outside." After I chuckled, I realized that he was serious. He followed up by saying, "Why do you think I come to the Camino for three months every two years?" It was in this moment that I realized that Roger's life was like that of many people – not all that he wanted it to be. And yet, he was showing up with genuine joy in his interactions with me. Yes, I know that people often fake their joy to cover up their sadness or lostness, but I could tell that Roger's joy was real. I felt it more than knew it.

Since I knew Roger's schedule, I knew that I had gotten ahead of him with my long walk into Santiago de Compostela on day six. I was certain that I'd never see him again. However, my decision to take a day off to rest (see Chapter 6) changed everything. Roger had shared with me that he expected to arrive in Santiago on June 1st, his birthday, and I had told Roger that my oldest son's birthday (Eric) was also on June 1. When I found myself still in Santiago on June 1st, I considered walking to Roger's albergue (he'd told me where he was staying) to buy him a beer for his birthday but decided against it because it was nearly a mile from where I was. While a mile might not seem like much, given the pain in my feet and legs it was too far, and I decided against it. But the universe had other plans.

Just Who

I was standing in downtown Santiago de Compostela (this city of over 100,000 people), and I was on the phone wishing my son Eric a happy birthday, when I heard someone say, "Jeff, Jeff" with a strong German accent. I looked up and saw Roger walking right in front of me. It turns out that he'd changed his plans and decided to stay somewhere very close to the heart of Santiago. I wished him a happy birthday and told him that I was on the phone with my son. Roger took my phone and shouted into it, "Happy Birthday Eric! Your father is the biggest man on the Camino. He is a giant!" Just pure joy. I asked Roger if he wanted to have dinner, and he agreed to come back to this area in thirty minutes. And Roger did come back.

In the interim, while I was still on the phone with my son, Tom (from Virginia) also walked by and we agreed to meet up for dinner (now the three of us). Later that evening Roger, Tom and I sat down for a beer at a table outside in the heart of Santiago and in the shadow of its great church. One beer quickly became two beers, and when Roger ordered his third beer (I was keeping up), Tom gave me a look that said it was too much. I told Tom that Roger loves his beer and that he (Tom) didn't have to keep drinking, but Tom kept up for the third and even the fourth beer. When we all decided that we needed to get something to eat, Roger recommended a tapas place just up the street. When we arrived at the restaurant Roger said, "First, we must have a shot," and proceeded to order whiskey shots for the three of us. It was a memorable evening and a beautiful celebration of friendship, connection and a Camino journey in the city of Santiago de Compostela. While I still had several days left on my journey (and Roger did as well, as he also was continuing to the sea), it was a special moment on my Camino journey and our picture is one of my favorites.

Three days later, my journey was over. I was in the oceanside town of Fisterra and was quickly walking to my ride back to Santiago to catch my flight. I had just walked out of the grocery store with a snack, and as I hustled to make my ride, I heard a familiar voice behind me shouting in a German accent, "Jeff, Jeff." Sure enough, Roger and I had found each other one last time. I had to hurry so I gave Roger a big hug, wished him well and blessed him on his Camino finish. It was the perfect ending to my Camino experience, and I left Roger feeling the same joy I had every time we had been together. Roger was my gift and lesson about joy – not about perfection in life, but about living with joy even through an imperfect and perhaps even flawed life experience. Thank you, Roger, for making me laugh on the Camino and for teaching me about joy.

I met many people on the Camino. Some for hours. Some for minutes. Some I learned parts of their stories. Some I didn't even learn their name. What we all had in common was a calling – all different, but all callings to be on this journey across northern Spain on the Camino de Santiago. I don't know why I met them all, but I know that each one gave me some gift (large or small) and that every interaction was genuine. There were no distracted conversations like the ones that sometimes happen here and in our day-to-day experiences. Even in the brief moments, we talked and shared openly and deeply. Perhaps, that's the nature of the Camino – thousands of people on their own personal journeys, but all sharing the common desire to be in this special place on a unique voyage of discovery.

> What we all had in common was a calling - all different, but all callings to be on this journey across northern Spain on the Camino de Santiago.

I'll share more stories of some of the people from my journey in this book, but I wanted to share the above core stories and people with you. They all played a significant role in my journey and experience, and I'm grateful for all of them and for everything they gifted me with on the Camino (whether intended or unintended). As you begin your journey through this book, I invite you to open yourself up to experience the magic of the Camino shared through the words, stories, people and pages that follow. Whether or not you ever have your own Camino experience, my hope is that what follows will fill you up with magic, wisdom and inspiration for wherever your journey takes you … *one step at a time!*

Chapter Five

Just Shake

*W*e all know about snow globes, whether from our childhood or from our adulthood, and they all have many things in common. First, they're generally round – thus, we call them snow *globes*. Second, they offer some idyllic scene, whether it be a building, a skyline, a mountain view, a farm scape, a holiday scene or even a beach (still confusing to me – who wants snow on a beach?). While there are differences – some are glass and some are plastic, some are light and some are heavy, some have music and others don't, some contain white snow and others contain sparkling snow – they all have one significant thing in common: the magic *only happens* when you shake it. Indeed, snow globes are made to be shaken, and without shaking them, they're just another pretty piece that sits on the shelf, the desk or the table. Yet snow globes have several powerful lessons to teach us which you can apply to your life and your leadership. And my Camino journey was the result of my conscious decision several years ago to shake up my life.

The Magic Is in the Shaking

What I've come to deeply understand and experience is that what's true for snow globes is also true of your lives, your leadership and your relationships – it's critical that you regularly shake your life snow globe. While looking good is nice, the snow globe's magic is in the shaking, and this is also true for every element of your life. In fact, a snow globe at rest is like your life at rest – *it looks good, but there's not much happening.* While you may think that a snow globe and life at rest are peaceful, the reality is that they're just settled. In fact, an apt description of a snow globe at rest is that it's not living up to its potential or what it was built to be and experience. The same is true for you and your life – without regular shaking, it's just okay and you're not living up to all you were built to be and experience.

To be clear, I'm not suggesting that change for the sake of change is a good thing, but a snow globe isn't about change. No matter how much you shake a snow globe, it doesn't change its essence – you only see things differently for a short period of time while the snow or sparkles are swirling. No, the shaking isn't the change – the shaking is designed to give you a new and different perspective about a situation, a challenge, an opportunity, a person, a relationship and even yourself. With this shaken up and different perspective you can then decide what (if any) changes to make in your beliefs, actions or both.

This book is about shaking, and it's intended to perform the act of shaking up your thinking and perspectives. The Camino certainly did that for me, and my decisions on how to experience the Camino were another form of shaking and staying in the uncomfortable. Ultimately, my hope and prayer is that this book will inspire you to shake up and shift your beliefs and actions so that you can transform your life, leadership, relationships and experience. Where do you need to shake things up in your life or leadership? What situation requires a shake and a fresh look? What relationships need to be shaken up for the benefit of both parties? What plan needs to not only be adjusted, but shaken up so you can clearly see what's working and what's not working once everything settles? If you want more magic in your life, then invite that magic by borrowing from the magic of snow globes. And remember this: *you've got to shake things to change things!*

If you want more magic in your life, then invite that magic by borrowing from the magic of snow globes. And remember this: *you've got to shake things to change things!*

Shake Regularly

Another lesson that I've learned is that no matter how long or how often you shake a snow globe, things quickly go back to normal, and this is a typical form of settling for many of us. Because snow globes are designed to look good even without the magic of shaking, after a minute or so they quickly *settle* into being just a nice-looking display piece. Similarly, when you shake things up in your life, your leadership, your team or your organization, you feel the magic, but it's fleeting and things quickly go back to the way they were before. In other words, they *settle* into what's comfortable.

We all know that it's easy to live comfortably in every aspect of our lives, and it's also easy to quickly revert back to the old normal (our comfort zones) after a brief shake-up. Perhaps you've read a book that filled you with new approaches and ideas. You might even have tried out some of these new actions for a brief time, but you quickly fell back to your old and comfortable ways. Perhaps you attended some training program and left it feeling on fire and ready to change the world (the shake-up), but then came everyday life, demands and distractions, and you ended up almost where you were before anything was shaken. This is why regularly shaking your life and leadership snow globe is so essential – to help you sustain and expand the momentum so that you can achieve real and lasting change in thinking, actions and outcomes.

My Camino journey was all about shaking – from the decision to go to the decision to not make reservations for places to stay. In choosing to never retrace my steps and go back, I was shaking my snow globe. In choosing not to become part of a Camino pilgrim group, I was shaking my snow globe. At every twist and turn it was more shaking, and that shaking made all the difference in Spain.

Not only is it critical to regularly shake up your snow globe but shaking your own snow globe is a fantastic act of modeling for everyone around you. Whether it's your partner, your family or your team, your act of snow globe shaking encourages and invites others to do the same. In addition, in any role where you can have a leadership impact, you can encourage others to shake their snow globes. In fact, you can even shake their snow globes for them in many ways.

One of the best ways to shake up the snow globes of the people you care about (whether it's your family, a partner or your team members) is to ask questions. High-quality and authentic questions serve us well in shaking our own snow globes and those of the people around us. Questions invite self-assessment, grow self-awareness, encourage personal responsibility and empower others to self-shake, self-shift and self-accelerate. While it's ultimately up to another person whether they actually change (yes, it's true – you can't change someone else), we all have the opportunity to shake other people's snow globes in various aspects of their lives. While there's always risk associated with the shaking – whether you're shaking your own snow globe or someone else's – that's the nature of personal and professional leadership. After all, nobody said that shaking things up was easy or risk free.

My final thought on regular snow globe and life shaking is this – if you don't regularly shake your own snow globe, other people, situations and life itself will shake it for you. That's the thing about snow globes – they're meant to be shaken, and your life is just the same. If you don't shake your own snow globe, you'll experience life as being out of control (as if someone or something else is shaking things up), and that's true. When you fail to shake things up on your own, then situations, experiences and people will create a shaken-up experience for you because you've given up control of your snow globe. In other words, you've become a victim of shaking rather than the victor of your own life and leadership shaking experiences.

The first step is to shake your personal life and leadership snow globe, and don't stop with one or just an occasional shaking. Once you shake your snow globe, keep regularly shaking it and pay close attention to what you see when your shaking creates a new and usually different perspective on whatever situation, challenge or opportunity is in front of you.

Watch Over Your Snow Globe

My friend Robin Sacks wrote a wonderful book called *Get Off My Bus!: How to Get Clarity, Get in the Driver's Seat, and Get Moving in Your Life!*

(Outskirts 2010), which encourages us all to get certain people off of our life bus – in other words, to stop letting yourself be surrounded by the people who discourage you, deplete you and get in your way. It's a simple and profound concept – getting people off your bus – and I recently realized that when you kick them off your bus you've got to do one more thing. You have to take back your snow globe.

If you're wondering how the hell these other people got their hands on *your snow globe*, the answer is simple and sad – *you gave it to them!* Yes, you heard me right – you've given your snow globe to other people, and most of you have also surrendered it to the vagaries of circumstances. By the way, in nearly every case you didn't consciously or intentionally give up your snow globe, but you did give it up.

Sometimes we give up our snow globes because we want to avoid personal responsibility for our lives and our outcomes. Sometimes we give them up because we're afraid. Sometimes we give them up because we're simply tired of being responsible. Many times we give up our snow globes to the people closest to us either because they asked us for them (usually unconsciously) or we believe that handing over our snow globes to someone else is an act of love or an investment in the relationship.

No matter what the cause or circumstances of you giving up and handing over your snow globe, it's time to reclaim your snow globe and to take personal responsibility for it and for its shaking.

No matter what the cause or circumstances of you giving up and handing over your snow globe, it's time to reclaim your snow globe and to take personal responsibility for it and for its shaking. If you're ready to re-empower yourself, to reclaim responsibility for your life, your impact and your outcomes, and to experience your life, leadership and relationships in different and deeper ways, then it's time to shake your snow globe. Not only now, but regularly because all perspective and outcome shifts start when you do this one thing – *Just Shake!*

Chapter 5

Just Listen

*A*s I shared at the outset of this book, my journey to the Camino began in a hotel in Raleigh in April of 2015, and little did I know how much that early awakening would serve as a wake-up call for me in my life. That beginning led me to meet and connect with many people who would guide and support me on along the way to the Camino. Shortly after watching *The Way*, I learned that a fellow speaker (Mark LeBlanc) had previously walked the Camino (twice) and that he'd written a book about his journey (*Never Be the Same*, 2010). I reached out to Mark to talk to him about his experience, but I never heard back from him. Then in July of 2016, the universe put Mark right in front of me at a fundraising auction as part of the National Speakers Association's annual conference in Phoenix, AZ. The Cigar PEG is a non-profit affiliated with the National Speakers Association, and members donate their services for an auction to raise money for the mission. You guessed it – Mark had donated a year-long coaching package for the auction.

I was interested in engaging a new coach, and given that Mark had walked the Camino, I was extremely interested in the coaching package. In addition, several of my friends there that night told me how amazing Mark was and encouraged me to bid. I told myself that I'd bid up to $5,000 for the coaching package, which was a financial stretch for me at the time. When the bid went over $5,000, I stopped bidding, and then the bidding came down to two people who had bid $6,000. As often happens at these charity auctions, they asked Mark if he was willing to donate two coaching packages for the two final bidders (neither of which was me). However, Mark did something unexpected and said, "I'll donate three coaching packages at $5,000 each." As soon as I heard it, my arm shot into the air, and thus began my journey with Mark LeBlanc.

When I talked to Mark that night, I told him that I looked forward to hearing about his Camino experience, and we started working together in September. In December of 2016, I traveled to Minneapolis to spend the weekend with Mark for an intense strategy, ideation and coaching session, and we spent a good bit of time talking about the Camino over dinner. One evening when I was having dinner with Mark and his wife, Ann, I was looking at a large picture of Mark on the Camino. Mark walked up to me and whispered in my ear, "You're going to do it." I asked Mark how he knew, and he said, "because the Camino has called you. I can see it in your eyes. People think that they choose the Camino, but the Camino chooses people, and you've been chosen."

In that moment, I felt a deep chill of excitement stir inside me, and I knew Mark was right – I didn't know why, but I knew I'd been chosen and I told myself that I would walk the Camino because I'd heard the call and I was listening.

In January of 2017, I sold my house, and I'd chosen not to decide where I'd go next until after I moved out of my house. I had planned to put nearly everything I owned into a storage locker and my "unplan" was to not have a permanent address – I'd split my time between Cleveland, OH, and Raleigh, NC, and just listen to be told where I was meant to be. When I talked to Mark in January, I had no specific plan to walk the Camino, and I'd just moved out of my house and was living with a friend who had offered a spare bedroom for my use. When I told Mark that I'd sold my house and had chosen to be a nomad, Mark said, "Why don't you walk the Camino with me in May?"

My heart leapt at this idea, and I immediately checked my calendar, where I found five speaking engagements in May that would keep me from journeying to the Camino with Mark (walking the entire 500-mile

Camino journey takes about 35-38 days including travel). This is when I had my first Camino shift as Mark shared with me that if you walk at least 100 kilometers (approximately sixty-two miles) on the Camino, and arrive in the destination city of Santiago, "You're official as a Camino pilgrim, and you'll go in the registry." What a shift – I'd thought that I could only have a Camino experience if I created more than a month of time to be away (and without income), and now I knew that I could make the experience happen with only seven to ten days. When I hung up with Mark, I made a commitment to myself and marked fifteen days on my calendar, leaving the day after my last speaking engagement in May. All because I'd just listened.

The next several months were filled with numerous synchronicities, including the following:

- On April 3, 2017, I woke up and decided to post my plans to walk the Camino on Facebook. When I opened Facebook to make the post, there was a Facebook memory from that **same date in 2015** – the morning that I'd posted about waking up in the hotel in Raleigh, watching the movie *The Way*, and knowing that I'd make the Camino journey.
- In April, I was talking to one of my leadership mentors (Phil Beverly) about some challenges I'd been facing – specifically, a feeling of aloneness – and he asked me if it would be possible for me to carve out some time away to just be alone. In response, I said "Do you mean like going to Spain to walk the Camino de Santiago for two weeks?" Phil responded by saying, "Are you kidding me? You already knew you needed to create time alone."
- About a month before leaving for Spain, I was having coffee with my good friend Craig James, and he mentioned that he and his wife Sue were going to be traveling in Europe in the spring and summer. When I asked him when, he said May and June. When I asked him where they were traveling, he listed several countries including France and Spain. When I

asked him where in Spain, he listed several cities including Madrid. When I pressed him on the dates of his travels to Madrid, we discovered that we were both flying to Madrid on the same date and arriving within an hour of each other. As a result, on my first night in Madrid I had dinner with two dear friends.

There are several other synchronicities that took place before I left for my Camino journey, and they all unfolded because I was willing to trust and to listen.

My first synchronicity on the Camino itself came the first night when I arrived in my starting city of Villafranca del Bierzo and discovered that my friend Mark LeBlanc was in the same city. We hadn't planned this, and Mark had planned to be further along on the Camino, but he'd chosen to rest by walking a short day. He didn't know that I was starting my journey in Villafranca until I texted him when I arrived. As a result, my experience began with dinner with Mark in Villafranca, and I still remember the joy and giddiness I felt sitting with him over dinner at an outdoor café on my first night on the Camino. This joy is radiating from Mark and me in the picture we took that night at dinner. I was so grateful that I'd listened.

So many synchronicities flowed from my openness and choice to listen to the people, opportunities and messages that were put in front of me. You too can experience the empowerment that just listening can deliver into every part of your life and leadership journey.

Are You Listening?

My question to you is simple – are you listening? So much (too much) of our lives is consumed with thinking about things and trying to figure things out, but I've learned that this rarely gets us where we're meant to be. I've realized that my fears, doubts and hesitations reside exclusively in my mind. Thus, when I try to think things through or figure things out, I'm relying on the part of me that's rational and afraid. Those voices you hear that say play it safe, don't take risks and be certain come from your thinking, but your deepest truths and knowing are in your heart, your spirit and your intuition, where it's vital that you just listen.

When I chose to be a nomad after selling my house in January of 2017, that came from listening, not planning and thinking. My theory was simple – how can I discern where I'm supposed to be when I'm still where I am? I just knew that I needed to be out of my old house and experiencing being free from that place and its history before I'd know where I was meant to be. I knew that meant just listening, which I did (including on my Camino journey), and this led to me deciding to purchase a condo in the Cleveland area after eight months as a nomad.

> Your deepest truths and knowing are in your heart, your spirit and your intuition, where it's vital that you just listen.

When I purchased the condo, people asked me about my thought process, and I told them that there was no thought process – I just listened in terms of the general area (Cleveland or elsewhere), the specific area and the home. The only thinking I did related to the financing terms – everything else was intuition and gut. When I walked into the condo I'd bought, I knew it was my place, and I said yes and made an offer. I just listened.

Ever since my Camino journey, just listening has become the norm for me, and it involves high levels of trust in myself and in my intuition. I've also realized that my thinking self is often confused and is working (unconsciously) to avoid risks, and sometimes it even tries to convince me that I don't deserve some outcome or experience. I'm guessing you know that feeling – the voice that doubts your worthiness in some way. Your thinking self is where that worthiness doubt lives, but your intuition and gut know your worthiness – they're the source of all that you truly are and deserve IF you're willing to trust and listen.

This past year I have continued to consistently trust and listen. I leapt by writing and publishing this book. I leapt by agreeing to lead a Mankind Project men's weekend in Ireland. I leapt by taking an epic trip to Alaska for a cruise with my entire family. I leapt by heavily investing in several marketing initiatives for my business. These are big leaps, but the biggest leap happened on Labor Day Weekend. After thirty-five years living in Cleveland, I sold my condo and moved to Tampa, FL to pursue a relationship even though the relationship was fairly new.

When I came to Tampa I knew one person here, and I'm now purposefully building a whole new network here (professional and personal). As part of this move, I also leapt into the Tampa Bay business community and various organizations. I've reached out to people that I know to ask, "Do you know anyone in the Tampa area that I should meet?" I've reached out to strangers that I've discovered on the Internet or who I saw across the room at a chamber meeting. All a part of trusting and listening.

No matter who you are or how present you are, leaping is still scary, and I've experienced every emotion this summer during my transition to Tampa. I've experienced joyful highs and sad lows. I've been angry and I've certainly been scared. And yes, I've doubted myself and wondered if I could do this (and felt shame in that doubt). Contrary to what people might believe about me and life, all emotions are natural – the only question is what I (and you) do with them.

There's no secret formula for listening – just a realization that all that you are and all that you're meant to be and experience will be revealed to you by listening (not by figuring things out). It also requires a readiness to trust yourself and your heart and soul voices more than you ever have before because you can sense (by listening) that that these voices are your truest and most authentic voices.

What things have you been trying to figure out while sensing (but not trusting) that there's an answer, a truth, calling to you? What are the things that you know you need to do (or stop doing), but you're choosing not to listen? Are you ready to trust yourself, your intuition and the answers that have always been waiting for you?

Just listening led me to my Camino journey and experience. Just listening led me to where I'm living today. Just listening leads my daily choices and experiences. Just listening is creating opportunities and outcomes in my business that I never imagined were possible. Just listening is allowing me to have a life experience filled with more joy, peace and love than I ever could have envisioned. Just listening has helped me to understand who I am and all that I'm meant to be. Just listening has allowed me to find forgiveness for others and, most important, self-forgiveness. Just listening is the way. Are you ready to just listen?

Chapter 6

Just Stop

As you know from this book's introduction, I literally limped into Santiago de Compostela and synchronistically connected with my friend Mark LeBlanc. Later that evening Mark and I had a lovely dinner in Santiago. We shared our Camino stories, experiences and lessons over dinner and a glass of wine. It was a magical evening. After dinner we limped (literally ... both of us) back to our hotel, and during the walk Mark asked me my plans for the next day. Mark was flying back home due to an illness in his family, but I was planning to continue my Camino journey all the way to the sea – what was once known as the end of the world – to the cities of Fisterra and Muxia.

Noting my serious limp, Mark suggested that I instead take a day off and rest in Santiago, and I responded that it would only be a fifteen-mile hike the next day (rather than my typical twenty miles per day). Mark again encouraged me to take a day off to rest. When I responded, "I'll be fine, and it's only fifteen miles," Mark asked me one of those questions that I'll never forget: "Do you do this in your life?" I knew immediately what he meant – he was asking if this was my regular experience and approach in life – to always push on, to always have it handled, to always overdo it, to always take on more rather than allow myself to rest. My answer was honest and immediate: "Yes, I do."

You see, this has long been my mode of living – pushing myself because I can and telling myself that it's just what needs to be done, yet I'm the one (through my choices) who creates this perceived need to push myself. This one day – in Santiago de Compostela – I chose differently, and I took the next day off to rest my body and my aching feet and legs. Not only was the rest much needed and amazing, but it allowed me to have some other synchronistic experiences that would have been impossible if I'd pushed on.

We live in a fast-paced world, and it's not slowing down. Yet each of us has the opportunity and the power to change this dynamic, and

The truth is that always doing is about worthiness, and this is what I've learned - I'm worthy enough to pause, slow down and even stop. And so are you.

it starts with the simple decision to just stop. The problem is that most of us keep telling ourselves that we can't stop or slow down because there's always so much to do. So much to accomplish. So much to get done. So much, so much, so much. I've discovered that there will always be more to do and that the push to always be doing and going has little to do with the things I think need to be done. The truth is that always doing is about worthiness, and this is what I've learned – I'm worthy enough to pause, slow down and even stop. And so are you.

My Superman Shadow

Carl Jung wrote about the shadow, and more recently the late author, speaker and coach Debbie Ford wrote extensively about this shadow concept. Shadow is said to be the parts of ourselves that we hide, repress and deny, and yet the voice of our shadow is the one that often drives our choices. One way to look at the shadow is as the inner voice that causes us to believe that we're not acceptable to our family, friends and, most important, ourselves. While we tell ourselves that we're good enough, the shadow quietly stalks us with a message that there's something wrong with us. It's usually some version of I'm not good enough – not loveable (my core shadow), not deserving, not pretty enough, not thin enough, not smart enough, not fun enough, not enough money … essentially, simply not worthy.

It's this voice – the voice of the shadow – that drives me to always be doing more – specifically, doing more than anyone else. I've named this shadow my Superman Shadow, which believes that I can (and must) do more than everyone else, go harder than everyone else, keep going when others would stop, etc. I'm now keenly aware that my Superman Shadow came into being because of my doubts about my worthiness. What about you? Can you relate to my Superman Shadow? What about your own shadow voices and doubts about your worthiness?

There are many different versions of the shadow voice in each of us, but the common theme is some form of unworthiness. Here are just a few examples:

Not smart enough
Not enough money
Not pretty enough
Not thin enough
Not funny enough
Not loveable
Not interesting enough
Not healthy enough
Not loveable *unless I* _____

The outcome of many of these shadow voices is the need to act or be a certain way in order to be accepted, to prove yourself or to be good enough. In many cases, the outcome is being externally driven to achieve. My Superman shadow is like this, and, while it may seem that being driven is a good thing, the better question is whether your version of being driven is healthy and overall serving you, your relationships and your life. Too many of us are living a driven life, but it's not a full life because our drive is flowing from our shadow voices. In other words, our driven nature is a way of silencing the shadow voices, but it's neither healthy nor authentic. In what ways are your worthiness doubts and questions showing up in your life, especially as it relates to constantly being busy and always doing? In what ways are your shadow voices driving you and your life, and what's the cost you're paying?

Always Pushing

I naturally have a great deal of energy and passion for and in my life, and this is not a bad thing, but it can be tricky when it comes to always going and my Superman Shadow. The problem isn't how much I work or how much I do, but why I do it. Is it driven by my desire to experience, to create and to impact, or is it driven by a subconscious need to outperform, outdo and out-go everyone else?

Here's a recent example of my life and schedule. I'd been traveling heavily (even for me) during a particular month – gone every weekend for four or five days for the entire month. The final trip was to Denver, CO, for a business-related boot camp, and I flew home on Saturday afternoon. A friend asked when I was traveling next, and I said that I was flying out the next morning to North Carolina for several days. When I returned from North Carolina, I was home for one day and then left town for a wedding. The following day I traveled another two and a half hours for an all-day meeting, and I was home for one day before leaving on a nine-day drive across the country. My friend's response to this schedule was, "I hope I have your energy when I'm 60 years old."

And that's when it hit me – I liked hearing that because I want people to see me as younger than my years and I want them to see me as having more energy than them. Why? Because having more energy than others is one way to compensate for the small but powerful inner voice that says, "I'm less than." Here's where my Superman Shadow can be tricky – am I doing so many things because I really love the experiences (which I do) or to fill some inside hole of less than? What I've learned is that I must be constantly vigilant to check in and see if my going is for me or just to feel better about myself. The answer determines whether my going and doing is part of my healthy life experience or if, instead, my Superman Shadow is running things and it's time to pause, slow down or just stop.

The Busy Epidemic

I give up words that don't serve me, and several years ago I decided to give up the word "busy." I did so because I realized that the concept of being busy is completely meaningless. Everyone is busy. People who have nothing to do are busy. Busy isn't descriptive; it's prescriptive. We have a deep need to be busy because the state of busyness has become the equivalent of value and worthiness. If you're busy, then you must be productive and valuable – or so you think.

When I tell people that I gave up the word "busy," they always want to know why, and then I explain it similarly to the above. When I'm asked what words I use instead, I tell people that I'm choosing to use words that are relevant, such as "I have a lot of good things I'm working on in my business," "I'm working on the right things or priorities," "I'm working on some new ideas," or "I'm being highly productive and profitable." One of the most often stated responses is some version of this: "Doesn't being busy mean that you're making money?" This always makes me laugh, and, if you're honest with yourself, you're also laughing because you know that being busy is easy and that it has nothing to do with being productive or profitable.

In this country we have an epidemic of busyness – everyone is busy, but few are being productive, prioritized or impactful. We're so busy being busy that we're missing out on friendships, parenting, relationships, interactions, intimacy and impact. There are even studies that suggest that we have to be busy in order to feel worthy. Author Brigid Schulte (*Overwhelmed: Work, Love and Play When No One Has the Time*, 2014) has written, "Somewhere around the end of the 20th century, busyness became not just a way of life but a badge of honor." Similarly, researcher Ann Burnett offers, "If you're busy, you're important. You're leading a full and worthy life." Sound or feel familiar? We're struggling with many addictions in this country, and the need to be constantly busy is perhaps the most ignored and devastating.

We're struggling with many addictions in this country, and the need to be constantly busy is perhaps the most ignored and devastating.

What Are You Afraid of?

Your first response is probably to say that you're not afraid of anything – you just have lots on your plate. But who put all of those things on your plate? One problem with our constant busyness is that we wrongly believe that we have no control over our plates or what goes on them. In fact, we all control our own plates, and we're the ones who are choosing to put so many things on our plates and in our lives. If you're like me, you're fabulous at saying "yes" and you struggle with saying "no" (whether it's to another person or just to a possible experience). What I've learned the hard way is that as challenging as "no" can be, every time I say "no" to someone else I'm saying "yes" to me. It's also a tangible expression of my worthiness – I'm worthy enough, and I don't have to say yes, do more, etc. to prove I'm worthy (usually to myself).

Part of the fear that drives constant busyness is that when we pause, slow down or stop we're left with just us. We're left to assess our worthiness based upon who we are rather than everything that we're doing, even if it's for others. Certainly, doing for others is often a good thing, and I'm a believer in giving of my time, treasure and talents, but the question is the why behind my giving and going. If I give my time so that you'll think better of me or so that I'll think better of myself, am I truly giving from the heart? Do you say "yes" because you're truly committed or because you're afraid to disappoint someone (and possibly because you're afraid that someone won't think well of you unless you say "yes")?

Stopping is particularly scary because when we stop we're left to face ourselves. For most of my life I couldn't be alone. I'm not talking about being extroverted – I'm talking about the almost insatiable need to be with other people, which was really an aversion to being alone. I know that many of you struggle with this challenge because many of my friends have told me precisely this: "I can't stand to be alone." It's because when you're alone you're left with just one person to trust, to share time with, to be intimate with, to be worthy enough – it's you. It's me.

Most of us have challenges in our lives, and it's only when we pause, slow down or even stop that we can really allow ourselves to feel the impact of these challenges. It's only when we slow down or stop that we can really learn about ourselves and find the path through our challenges (rather than hiding from them and the pain by constantly going).

Constant going is one key way to avoid facing our challenges, facing our fears, facing our pain, facing our lives, facing ourselves. No wonder slowing down is so frightening and seen as something to be avoided.

I vividly remember the gut-wrenching feeling I had when Mark lovingly challenged me with his **question**: "Do you do this in your life?" That feeling in my gut is what I know to be a truth response – my gut, heart and intuition telling me that I absolutely do this all the time in my life. I go and go and go, and I don't want to slow down or stop – not because of what I want, but because of what I want to avoid: the feeling that I'm not enough, that I'm not young enough, that I'm just like everyone else. Nothing special – not superman.

You Don't Have to Prove Anything

Much like the fear of slowing down, always being in action, always doing and going, and always doing more and more and more is a form of trying to prove something. Trying to prove to others that you're good enough, but more deeply trying to prove to yourself that you're good enough and worthy enough. Trying to prove that you're valuable. Does this sound or feel familiar for you?

If you're thinking that this isn't true about you, think about this question – when you do so much and are always going, do you do it silently or do you make sure that people know how much you're doing? When people ask you how things are, do you tell them about a few interesting things you're working on or some recent experiences? Or do you instead tell them how busy you are, how full your plate is and how crazy your schedule is? If you're not trying to prove anything to anyone, then why are you telling everyone about your fast-paced and full life? Gotcha!

It's time to be honest with yourself – most of us feel some need to prove ourselves to others (and to ourselves) by always doing, by always going, by always saying "yes." And always saying yes to others means always saying no to you – and to the people, things and experiences you want and deserve. It's time to say yes to someone incredibly worthy and special – it's time to say yes to you.

You're Worthy Enough to Stop

The simplest truth I can share with you, which was brought home to me by Mark's simple question in Santiago, is this – you ARE worthy enough to pause, to slow down and even to stop. Who you are isn't defined or determined by how much you do, how hard you work and how full your schedule is. What you already know is this – having a full schedule doesn't

You ARE worthy enough to pause, to slow down and even to stop.

equate to having a full heart or a full life! It's just a full schedule, and that full schedule often leaves you with an empty heart and life.

There are so many gifts we receive when we choose to pause, slow down or stop. When I chose to stop in Santiago, I received the gift of rest, relaxation and rejuvenation that my mind, body and spirit deeply needed. I had the opportunity to explore the beautiful city of Santiago de Compostela and to see things I'd never have seen if I'd pressed on. As I shared with you earlier, I was also gifted with dinner with two of my Camino friends (Roger and Tom, whom I'd met along the way), which only happened because I decided to stop.

I've learned that life often gives me similar gifts when I choose to pause, to slow down, or to stop. I have the opportunity to rest my body, my mind and even my soul. I allow myself to restore and rejuvenate every part of me. I allow myself to just be instead of always doing. I allow myself to experience different things and to experience them more deeply. Relationships are better and deeper. I experience more intimacy in every aspect of my life. I'm more present in every situation and with every person in my life. I'm more productive, effective and impactful. My business is more consistent and more profitable. My work with my clients is more impactful and meaningful. All because I choose to slow down and sometimes to even stop.

Yes, there are still times that I'm going and doing, but I've learned to slow down and to stop on a regular basis. More important, I've learned that I'm worthy enough to slow down and to stop. I'm worthy enough to say "no" or "not now." I trust that I'm worthy enough without having to go or do. I've learned that my Superman Shadow isn't the essence of who I am – it's a creation of that part of me that doubts my worthiness – and I'm choosing to take off the cape and just be Jeff.

The same is true for all of you. You're already enough. You're worthy enough to say "no." You're worthy enough to pause, to slow down, to stop. You're more than enough without doing and doing, and without going and going. There are many amazing parts of your true self that you've not yet discovered and which you've not yet shared with others (and even the world), and we're waiting for you. It's time to give the world the gift of you, and all you have to do is *Just Stop*.

Chapter 7

Just Love

On January 15, 2018, less than a year after my Camino journey, Sandra Nischwitz (Mom) took her last breath. It wasn't expected, but her health had been fragile since her stroke four years earlier, and she went downhill quickly. Mom was 80 years old, and I realized many months after her death that Mom was my biggest fan. She loved my travels and adventures, and every phone call was sure to start with this question from Mom: "Where are you?" And I always looked forward to sharing my whereabouts with Mom.

When I'd visit her, the staff at her assisted living facility would always ask me, "Are you the son that's always traveling?" After my Camino journey, the staff would ask, "Are you the son that went on that long walk?" I waited a long time before I told Mom about my decision to travel to Spain to walk the Camino for one reason – Mom was a worrier. I figured the later I told her, the less time she'd have to worry. However, she surprised me when I told her about my upcoming trip because she didn't express any concerns about my safety (usually her big thing). Instead, she expressed delight and encouragement. I don't know if Mom was being honest or just being polite, but either way it was great to have her support as I prepared for the Camino.

Mom traveled a great deal across the country when my Dad was playing professional baseball, but her only international travel had been to

Canada and Japan when I was very young. She'd never been to Europe, so I think she was genuinely excited about my Camino trip. I was also blessed to travel back to Europe later in 2017, and Mom was equally excited for me and about my adventures. I made a point to regularly call Mom from my various destinations in 2017, including a memorable call to her when I was walking the streets of Paris. I think she got a big kick out of that call. I know I did.

2018 was filled with a great deal of sadness at losing Mom, as well as two uncles. Another uncle had passed away when I was on the Camino. When I got the call to come to be with my Mom for her last days, I was spending the weekend with a small group of friends (all men), and they blessed me in incredible ways before I began my journey to Dayton, OH to be with Mom. What I remember most about that interaction was these words from my friend Claude: "Soon your life will change forever, and you'll begin the next part of your life as a motherless son." Those words were important to hear and have comforted me since Mom took her last, beautiful breath. And it truly was beautiful.

When we were called into her room because "it was time," my brother, sister-in-law, sister and I were gathered around Mom's bed – witnessing, crying, holding, trusting. I remember the moment when Mom took her last breath, and as I wept at her passing, it struck me that Mom and I had been together since my beginning. She was there when I took my first breath, and I was blessed to be there when she took her last breath. In the midst of my deep sadness and grief in that moment, it also struck me how simple and peaceful her last breath had been.

No more pain for her. No more sadness for her. No more grief for her (having already lost a son, a marriage, family members, and many friends). No more uncertainty. No more less than full living since her stroke. Just peace. As the tears poured out of me, I realized that in the exact same moment I was experiencing profound joy for my Mom's peace and the witnessing of that last breath. Divine proof that joy and sadness (like all emotions) can exist in the precisely same moment. No either / or, but both / and. I'll never forget that moment.

You may be wondering what all of this has to do with my Camino journey and about love, and that's the magic of it all. When I was with my Mom in her last twenty-four hours, I had the opportunity to talk with many of the staff at her facility. One staff member (who also asked if I was the son who took the long walk) told me that Mom had told her that I was going back to the Camino (which I am) and that she (Mom) planned to go with me. When the staff member told her that she better get out of her wheelchair and get in shape, Mom apparently got testy and told her very clearly, "I'll be with him." Clearly, Mom already knew and had already made her plans to be with me when I go back to the Camino, and I'm looking forward to having her with me again and in even more meaningful ways.

What was even more profound for me was all the people (staff, friends and other residents) who talked to my brother, sister and me during those last days. They all wanted to share stories of Mom with us, and more than just stories, memories of the impact Mom had on them and in their lives. I especially remember one aide who wasn't working, but someone let her know that Mom was in her final hours (something they weren't allowed to do, by the way), and she made a point to come visit Mom. Mom hadn't been responsive for about twenty-four hours, but all of us were talking with her. As I listened to this young woman talk, saying thank you to Mom, I discovered something special and magical about Mom – how much and how well she just loved. We heard dozens of these stories over that week.

I already knew that Mom was someone who always had a smile on her face (and a butterfly pin on her top), and she was always known as being a very positive person. What a few of us knew is that her outward appearance of positivity was a mask – a mask that covered up her sadness, grief and even depression. Mom always brought a brightness into a room and into her interactions with others, but I'd never really understood (until the end) the many ways that Mom loved others – perhaps even more deeply over the last four years of her life than ever before. I was grateful to have been gifted with the many love stories that people shared with us – what I'm now calling *just love* stories.

What I've realized and learned from this experience is that there are four elements of the love that Mom gifted to so many people during her life. They're simple and profound:

1. See Them
2. Accept Them
3. Believe in Them
4. Bless Them

The rest of this chapter is committed to sharing with you the ways that Mom loved so many, and my hope is that each of you will pick up where Mom left off – that you'll embrace these simple ways of loving the people around you, whether it be family, friends, partners or team members – that you'll just love!

See Them

You would think that this element of loving others – seeing them – would be easy, but this involves so much more than physically seeing people. It requires a commitment to and openness towards others. It requires that

My hope is that each of you will pick up where Mom left off - that you'll embrace these simple ways of loving the people around you, whether it be family, friends, partners or team members - that you'll just love!

you acknowledge and listen to them and that you take a genuine interest in them and in their lives, including caring enough to remember them and the intimate parts of their lives they share. Unfortunately, we live in a world that's so fast-paced, so full of activities and so full of distractions that seeing people isn't as natural or as easy as it sounds. And seeing others is just the beginning of loving others.

While people will often share themselves with us, this usually comes only after they sense a level of genuine interest, and the best way to communicate this interest is to ask questions. Our culture has devolved to one that's fascinated with talking and telling, and questions have taken a back seat in our communication. Personally, I love (even treasure) questions and see them as the most powerful communication, connection and relationship building tool we have. Yes, I know that's a big statement, but it's true.

Questions are the gateway to learning, to understanding, to discovery, to creation, to empathy, to compassion, and even to healing. While learning to be a questioner involves intention, it also requires science (skills), art (intuitive listening) and a genuine interest in people – all people, and their lives. It also demands that we create an environment where people feel safe enough to share themselves – to allow you to *see them*.

Being seen is an odd thing in that we all have a deep need to be seen (and accepted), and at the same time there's a risk in being seen because it involves being vulnerable and exposed to possible judgment and even rejection if we're truly and authentically seen. That's one of Mom's magic elements of loving others because she created that safe space using many of the other *just love* elements (especially acceptance).

When we talk about asking questions, listening, caring and being genuinely interested, we're not talking about the information of people's lives. We're talking about the *stories* of their lives – the good, the bad and the ugly, the uncertainties, fears and doubts, the wins and losses, the ups and downs – essentially, the truth of their lives and their experiences of their lives. This is something that Mom was brilliant at – drawing out people's stories.

Mom was a storyteller and a grand story listener. She loved hearing people's stories and cherished them (both the stories and the people). There's a word we don't hear or use much: cherished. Mom cherished people, including the time she spent being with them, talking to them, listening to them, and encouraging them. I know all of this is why we created a cemetery marker for Mom which has the following words inscribed on the marker because they're so true about Mom:

"Loving Mom, Wife, Grandma, Caring Friend,
Sharer of Smiles and Lifter of Spirits"

Certainly, an impactful legacy from life.

Recently, my friend Nick Gargala shared this wisdom with me about life and death: there are three deaths. First, when our body dies. Second, when we go to our final resting place (either burial or cremation). Third, the last time our name is spoken. Talk about legacy. I know Mom's name will continue to be spoken for generations and generations, and not because of what she accomplished, what she earned, or even for the family she raised. Mom's legacy will be in the lives she touched through simple acts of love – by just loving the people around her.

Mom saw the people around her, and in fact she went out of her way to see them, to listen to them, to share with them, and to experience them. Are you living your life this same way? Are you committed enough, and do you care enough to see people? Or are you in a hurry with a full plate and a full life? Do you make time for people and their stories, or are you moving so fast that you can only find time for a few bits of information?

Children grow up starving to be seen, and that need continues (and often grows) as we move into adulthood. Think about people and leaders you know who always seem to be talking (even over-talking), who are always front and center, who seem to be almost waving their arms and yelling "look at me" or "see me." We often think of this behavior as being arrogant, but I suspect it's just the opposite – a desperate call to be seen, to be acknowledged, to be heard. Mom made sure that the people around her were seen, acknowledged and heard. She remembered them, their information and their stories. She cared enough. She loved them.

Are you willing to live and love the same way? Are you willing to slow down enough to enthusiastically seek out and listen to people's stories? Are you willing to make time for stories and experiences? Are you willing to make a new or renewed commitment to seeing people, being genuinely interested in them and their stories? Perhaps most important, can you find the place inside yourself to cherish people, their stories and their lives? They just want to be seen. Mom saw them, and this seeing formed a connection that went beyond friendship, one that can't even be defeated by death. Mom is gone, but life goes on and, most important, love goes on, and on, and on, and on. Will you just see them?

> Mom saw them, and this seeing formed a connection that went beyond friendship, one that can't even be defeated by death.

Accept Them

As challenging as seeing others can be (simple but challenging given the speed and state of our culture and relationships), this next love element is even more challenging because it requires us to turn off one of our most natural reactions. In order to accept people, you have to be willing and able to not judge them. That's right – to turn off your judgments and accept people as they are and where they are. As I'll share more below, this doesn't mean that we agree with everyone or that we stay silent if we disagree. In fact, loving someone often means telling them the truth about what you see in them, in their life and in their choices, but being honest with someone doesn't mean judging them. In the simplest terms, this is the key element for creating a safe place for people to share and be vulnerable, and the shortest way to describe this love is one word – unconditional.

As you're reading this, you may already be starting to feel uneasy, and that response is natural. Whether you want to admit it or not, judging others (and their choices) is the cultural norm today and has been for thousands of years. We've been trained and almost bred to judge others, but there's a place between disagreeing and judgment that is the domain of acceptance and unconditional love. Seeing or hearing people making decisions differently than you would, but still accepting and loving them. Seeing issues and the world differently than someone else, but still accepting and loving them. Knowing that people are living their lives differently than you choose to live life – and holding different beliefs – but still accepting and loving them. Interacting with people who look different from you and still accepting and loving them. This was one of Mom's gifts to all of us.

I can't say that Mom was always this way, accepting and non-judgmental. In fact, there were several times in our relationship over the years when Mom did judge others, including me. One of my and our most difficult times was when I'd made some bad choices in my life. I didn't really see the choices that way then (at least not the way Mom did), but I was aware of my choices and the damaging impact they'd had on my family – choices around my marriage, around fidelity, around my wife – and Mom did judge me. I remember a phone call when Mom called to belatedly congratulate me on publishing my first book, and she said, "I'm proud of you for writing this book. I know it took a lot of work. I'm not proud of you in many ways, but I should have let you know about the book months ago." I certainly felt judged, and I'm guessing that Mom would acknowledge the judgment, but our relationship recovered and, as I said above, Mom became my biggest supporter and fan. I think in many ways Mom changed later in her life – she dropped her judging tendency, or perhaps her judgments were limited to those closest to her.

Whatever the case or the reasons, Mom accepted people, their lives and their choices, and at the same time she challenged them and questioned them. Over the last four or five years of Mom's life, she was more honest with people than she'd been earlier in life. Perhaps she felt the need to pretend or be silent earlier, but she didn't hold back in her last few years. Mom seemed to master the paradox of disagreeing with someone without judging them, and that mastery served her well in being willing (a key start) and able to put down her judgments and love people as they are – to accept them.

Where are you judging in your life and your many relationships? You can be assured that these judgments are having an adverse impact on not only your relationships, but your leadership, your impact and your joy. While we may have some fears about vulnerability, we all crave deeper levels of intimacy in our lives and relationships, and that intimacy can't coexist with judgments. Now is probably the best time to share a distinction that's essential in living life without (or with fewer) judgments, and I'm talking about discernment. Choosing not to judge doesn't mean changing your beliefs or not seeing differences, but it does mean a change in what we do with the differences and disagreements.

The easiest way to explain this difference is this – It's one thing to see someone or their choices as different (discernment) but It's something very different to make judgments about that person as *less than or inferior* because of the differences (judgment). I'm not suggesting that you have to or even should give up your discernments – they're important in so many different ways, including living according to your personal values and setting boundaries. What I am suggesting is that loving people requires you to put down or minimize your judgments, even if this only happens in small steps and increments.

There was a time when I struggled with the concept of unconditional love and thought (and was told by many others) that it meant accepting whatever someone else says or does to me and allowing it to continue. This is particularly relevant in relationships, which can sometimes become unhealthy and even toxic. I thought that unconditional love meant accepting whatever someone else does, but now I see that there's a difference between unconditional love (non-judgment) and unconditional relationship (failing to discern and take care of myself). A great example of unconditional relationship is being in and choosing to stay in a relationship (romantic, friendship or work) where you're subjected to physical, emotional, sexual or mental abuse. You can love someone unconditionally and still choose not to accept their behaviors, especially when their choices and actions have a very real impact on you and in your life.

I know Mom didn't agree with everyone she met and interacted with, and I'm confident she disagreed with people's choices. However, Mom chose (and it is a choice) to continue to accept people, including their differences and their choices, without judgment, all while challenging them, asking questions and I'm sure, giving advice. These were and are acts of love and acceptance, and they flow from the intentions you set and the choices you make in your relationships and interactions with other people.

> You can love someone unconditionally and still choose not to accept their behaviors, especially when their choices and actions have a very real impact on you and in your life.

Are you ready to accept? Are you ready to drop (or at least diminish) your judgments? You'll likely have to start by acknowledging your judgments and your judging nature. For a culture that claims to not be judgmental (most people say that they're not judging or judgmental), we're certainly a judging culture. You can't change the ways you interact with and accept others unless and until you're willing to own your judgments – to catch yourself at first and put down your judgments as you move into a less and less judging experience with others. Think about how you feel when you experience the judgments of others and also how good it feels to be accepted, even if you're different from or believe different things than other people. That feeling of acceptance, of unconditional love, is a core ingredient of loving others and feeling loved, and we can all use a whole lot more of that experience in our lives. Mom gave this gift to others, and you can choose to give this loving gift as well if you're ready and willing to just love.

Believe in Them

While Mom's passing has been difficult and has left me with an emptiness that will likely last until my last breath, there have been many incredible gifts that resulted from her death. One of the most impactful for me came in the form of my oldest son, Eric, and his eulogy at Mom's funeral service. Eric is the oldest of Mom's grandchildren, and he decided to speak at the funeral, which in some ways surprised me, but in many ways it did not. What I wasn't prepared for, however, was the power and impact of his message and words. Without any notes or outline and starting with a simple message, Eric delivered a moving eulogy that not only spoke volumes about Mom's loving spirit, but inspired everyone in the room to be, live and lead differently. And at the heart of his message was the theme of believing in people.

There were two words that flowed throughout Eric's story and message about his grandma – "Well sure!" Eric told several stories about the times when he told his grandmother about things he wanted to do, experience or achieve, and her answer was always the same: "Well sure!" Her meaning was clear to Eric and all of us who heard Eric's message that day – of course you can, and of course you will. As Eric explained, it didn't matter how crazy or seemingly unrealistic the plan was, Mom's answer was always a resounding, supportive and encouraging "Well sure!" "Well sure you can," "Well sure you will" or "Well sure that will happen." While Eric's stories and Mom's words were meaningful, it was Eric's sharing of the impact of Mom's words and support on him that touched me.

Eric tearfully shared this: "When Grandma told me 'well sure,' it showed me that she believed in me, and it helped me to believe in myself. That's the gift that Grandma gave me and lots of other people." There it is – the game changer – helping people believe in themselves by *believing in them*, and that's precisely what Mom did as part of her *just loving* them.

In Mom's last days, my family and I were gifted with many stories of people in Mom's life who were impacted by her simple words and acts of believing in them. Certainly, it all started with her seeing them and also accepting them, but the act of letting people know that you believe in them and their dreams goes far beyond seeing and accepting. Mom not only listened to their stories, goals and dreams, but she remembered them and would regularly ask them where they were on the path to those dreams.

It was common for Mom to ask people if they'd started on the path to their goal, whether it was education, training, starting, fixing or ending a relationship, healing a friendship, doing something with their children, or taking a trip. Mom listened, remembered, reminded and gently (i.e. lovingly) pushed people to believe in themselves because she genuinely believed in them. You can't fake believing in someone – it has to come from the heart, which is why it's an act of love. Mom believed in people and made sure they experienced that belief through her words,

All of this helped those people believe in themselves, which is perhaps the greatest gift we can give to another human being.

her actions, her reminders and her memory of those goals and dreams. All of this helped those people believe in themselves, which is perhaps the greatest gift we can give to another human being.

Do you believe in people, especially the people close to you? Do they know it? Is your belief unconditional or is it conditional on whether or not you agree with their goals and dreams? While it's okay to ask challenging questions, do your questions come in the form of I believe in you and your dreams and here are some things to think about, or are you quick to tell them all the reasons that something will not work, will not happen or that they can't do it? Or perhaps you're the type of person that wants to protect people, so you encourage them to be realistic ("Don't get your hopes up"). Protecting people can feel and seem loving, but who are you protecting? Are you protecting them, or are you really speaking to them from your own fears and doubts? Have you been disappointed and thus you want to keep them from being disappointed?

Love comes in different forms, but it's easy to fall into the trap of doing what you think is best to keep people safe from disappointment and, in the process, squashing their dreams and hearts. People are starving for someone to believe in them and to believe that they have whatever it takes to achieve their goals and dreams, whether big or small. Mom fed people in her life with a heart for believing in others and with just two words – *Well sure!*

Are you feeding the people in your life with words of encouragement and support, or are you focused on keeping them safe according to your own view of the world and how you *think* it works or doesn't work? If you want to love the people that cross your path in life, I invite you to be clear about the words you share, the support and encouragement you offer (or don't) and whether you're focused on them or on yourself. My hope is that you'll be a giver and nurturer of hope by believing in people and thereby helping them to believe in themselves.

Think of it this way – while being realistic is sometimes good counsel, this world doesn't need another naysayer. People of this world don't need someone else to tell them to be cautious, to be realistic and to not get their hopes up. Perhaps one reason we struggle with having hope is that we haven't been filled up with words of hope. It's time for us all to be believed in and to more deeply believe in ourselves. Mom must have known this, and she gifted hundreds or more by believing in them. Will you believe in them?

Bless Them

When was the last time you were given a blessing? When was the last time you gave someone a blessing? I'm not talking about giving a blessing before a meal or at an event – I'm talking about words or actions that bless another person. I'm guessing your answer was either never, I can't remember or not very often. Sadly, this is the reality of our world today in that we fail to bless others and ourselves – largely because we were never or rarely blessed ourselves. Whether it's at home, in relationships or at work, people are starving to be blessed and often don't even know that they're starving. Whether Mom set an intention to bless or not, it came naturally to her, and blessing others was another key part of her *just loving* them.

Let's start with what a blessing is, keeping in mind that it often doesn't, and doesn't need to, include the word blessing. Blessing is about an intention that includes some of the elements listed above – seeing them, accepting them and believing in them – and it's a way to let people know that the foregoing is true about them. Think about a time that you felt blessed by a person, situation or experience. I'm guessing that there was some element related to being worthy enough. Think of this often-used phrase: "I can't believe that I'm so blessed." If we can't believe it, then we're questioning whether we deserve or are worthy of the words, outcomes or experiences that we're encountering. Feeling blessed can also be a form of humility in honoring God, the Universe or some other higher power (or karma) for something that happened for you or to you. I wonder, however, whether we're most likely to attribute outcomes and experiences *to luck or to being blessed*?

In ancient times, people went to the rulers or spiritual leaders for a blessing, and receiving such a blessing was considered special and often sacred. In many religious groups and practices, there are ritualistic forms of blessings (e.g. marriage or baptism); however, the act of giving and receiving a blessing isn't limited to rulers and religious leaders. We can give and receive blessings every day, but we do have to set an intention, we do have to pay attention, we do have to see people and we do have to take the time to thoughtfully give the blessing.

Here are several key elements to blessing others:

- **Intention** – As already noted above, blessing someone else is often more about the intention than about the actual words or actions.

- **Be Specific** – As I'll explain further below, a blessing must be specific, which lets someone know that you've really seen them.
- **Impact** – When we share information or data with people, we communicate, but the act of blessing someone goes beyond the data, which results in a profound and often emotional impact on the person receiving the blessing (if they're able to receive it).

All of these elements are the essence of blessings, as the following examples will highlight and amplify.

While blessing someone in the workplace may seem like an odd concept, it's the most impactful way to empower, engage and inspire your team members, whether you're a designated leader or not. We might call this part of the praise and appreciation process (i.e. feedback), but blessing a team member goes far beyond what we typically consider praise. Let's compare words of praise versus words of blessing at work.

Praise: "Great job," "Thanks for all your hard work," "Appreciate your efforts on this project," "Glad to have you on our team."

Blessing: "I want you to know that I really appreciate the way you handled and led this project. Not only did we have a favorable outcome, but there were several times when the team started to get off course and you got everyone back online while keeping them engaged. I also appreciate the way you got the entire team involved with the project so that everyone felt included and contributed. Thank you for making everyone better."

Hopefully, the difference is obvious. This blessing message has all of the elements listed above. Such an empowering message follows from a blessing intention, it's specific (evidencing that you're really seeing the person and their efforts), and the message goes far beyond data or information and includes the positive impacts from their actions and leadership.

Here's what I've learned about blessing others – it's so powerful and rare that many people have a difficult time receiving it, but that's not a reason to withhold blessings. I often do role playing around blessings when I'm speaking, and here are some typical responses I hear from the people receiving the blessing from me (remember, this is role playing, so the blessing is made up):

"I've never received anything like that before, and it was difficult to receive."

"I'm feeling emotionally overwhelmed by your words, almost to the point of tears."

"I'd love to hear those kinds of words from my boss, even once."

How sad it is that these types of blessings in the workplace are absent or, at best, rare! It's all about a lack of awareness and intention. It doesn't take much more time to give a blessing, but it does take more presence, intention and attention – to really see people and their contributions so that you can bless them with specific, supportive and empowering words. And if you're wondering whether blessings should be saved for special or extraordinary efforts, I'll ask you this in return – why would you withhold a blessing of a small thing and save it for a big thing? If you're worried about people coming to expect blessings or other people being jealous if they don't receive one, that just means that you've got to be even more attentive and intentional in seeing people and blessing them even for the small stuff.

Blessings are a gift to give and to receive, and we don't need to limit them – we're already doing that. We need to set our intentions and become blessers of others, just like Mom. This is what Mom did regularly for the people that she interacted with. It didn't have to be and often wasn't some big effort or event – Mom blessed people for their small acts of care, attention or

> Blessings are a gift to give and to receive, and we don't need to limit them - we're already doing that. We need to set our intentions and become blessers of others, just like Mom.

kindness. These blessings – acts of love – helped people to believe in themselves, to feel worthy and to be ready in turn to give these blessings and love to others. Wow – what a ripple effect that comes from blessing others!

Let's take a look at another example of praise versus a blessing, this time with our children.

> **Praise:** "Nice game today," "Nice hit / catch" or "Good report card"
> **Blessing:** "I loved watching you play today. It excites me to see you having fun, and I especially like the way you support and encourage your teammates. I can see how you're a leader in the little things that you do. I especially love seeing you smile when you're playing. I look forward to seeing you continue to have fun at future games." OR "I really appreciate all the effort you put into your studies and school work, and It's great to see your hard work pay off. I'm proud of you – not for the grades, but for the way you're making your education a priority. Keep up the good work and let me know if I can support you in any way."

Once again, this difference is far beyond words, and it follows from a blessing intention. The blessings are specific, go beyond the mere information (or results) and encourage the child for who they are and for the experience, not just the outcomes.

By now I hope that the beauty and impact of blessing others is clear to you, as well as the need for more blessing intentions, actions and words in our organizations and with our teams, families and relationships. While some people will struggle initially in receiving blessings, this is a struggle worth creating because the ultimate gift and impact is worth the initial discomfort in receiving. I also know that when people are regularly blessed, they bless others, who then bless others, and on and on. You can be part of creating a ripple and then a wave of blessing by setting the intention and just starting.

Richard Carlson is famous for his wide series of books that started with *Don't Sweat the Small Stuff ... and it's all small stuff* (Hachette Books

1996), but when it comes to blessings it's about the small stuff. Bless the small stuff and you'll create some of the big stuff such as confidence, empowerment, worthiness, boldness and leadership. Blessing others is a small investment with massive returns, if you're willing be the blesser that they've been waiting for and if you're willing to just love them.

Just Love Them

The day Mom died was a sad day, and I know that I'll continue to experience moments and times of this sadness the rest of my days, but Mom's passing gave me a gift – the gift of really understanding Mom's core as a leader. That core was loving others and thereby helping others to believe in themselves, to see beyond their perceived limitations and to push past some of their (often self-limiting) stories about themselves and about life. Honestly, I never thought of my Mom as a leader during her life. I saw her as someone who took care of stuff, helped out all the time, cheered people up and was always at the ready with a smile. I also knew that much of Mom's life had been about loss, grief and depression, but I'd missed much of the essence of Mom's leadership and impact until her death.

Now I see it so clearly, and Mom's legacy is secured through the simple commitment (put into action) to *Just Love Them*. I know Mom touched, empowered and impacted many people and lives, and that impact will live on for generations because many of the people that Mom just loved will do the same to others. One of those people she touched and impacted was me, including on my Camino journey. She walked with me in spirit and in my heart. She shared in the journey in deep and joyful ways and shared that joy with many people who crossed her path.

If you want to deeply transform not only the lives of people around you, but your own life's journey, take note of Mom's message to us all – just love them! My hope is that each one of you will choose to live and love this way, and I know that your choice put into action will build upon and expand possibilities and hope. If you want to be the change you want to see in the world, it's quite simple – Just Love Them!

Chapter 8

Just Let Go

*T*here's a fabulous tradition and ritual on the Camino that involves stones and the Iron Cross. The Iron Cross (aka Cruz de Fierro) is located at the highest point of the Camino de Santiago, on Mount Irago within the Leon Mountains. On a large mound of stones left by Camino pilgrims is a tall oak pole topped with an iron cross. The pilgrim tradition is hundreds of years old and involves each pilgrim carrying a stone from their starting point (or from home) and leaving it in the pile of stones at the base of the Iron Cross. The leaving of the stone represents letting go of something, perhaps atoning for a sin or some other form of release.

When I saw this ritual in the movie *The Way*, I knew that it would be part of my Camino journey. I shared this ritual with several friends before I left for Spain, and they asked me to carry and leave stones for them as a way of them letting go of something in their life or thinking. I also had my own stones (I brought two stones with me) to represent the letting go of things that were holding me back in my life. I was so excited about being a part of this ritual and living it on the Camino. And then I learned an important lesson about movies – *they're often not accurate.*

Yes, there most certainly is an Iron Cross on the Camino. Yes, Camino pilgrims leave stones in the large pile around the Iron Cross. Yes, the ritual is real. And no, the Iron Cross isn't at the end of the Camino as depicted in *The Way*. At dinner on my first night on the Camino I was speaking to my pilgrim mentor Mark, and I told him of my excitement about leaving the stones I was carrying at the Iron Cross. My excitement quickly faded when Mark informed me that the Iron Cross was earlier on the Camino – a couple of days' walk *before* the spot where I'd started my Camino journey. While my disappointment was immediate, it didn't last because I promptly shifted from impossibilities (I wasn't going to walk back several days for the Iron Cross) to new possibilities (the end of the world).

While the official ending of the Camino is the city of Santiago de Compostela, you can choose to continue your Camino journey and walk on to one of two (or both) towns on the Atlantic Ocean – Fisterra and Muxia. I was already planning to walk on to both of these coastal towns, and Fisterra has long been known as the end of the world. In Roman times, this peninsula was believed to be the end of the known world (remember the world was once thought to be flat), and the Latin origin of the town's name comes from "end of the earth." What better place (perhaps even better than the Iron Cross) to let something go than by throwing the stone and what it stands for into the Atlantic Ocean at the "end of the world." And so, with my new mission, I was ready to continue my Camino journey with the clear intention to let go of some thoughts, beliefs and even relationships that were holding me back. It was time to let go!

The next morning (my second morning on the Camino), I woke up to a text from my brother Brad letting me know that my Uncle Chuck had passed away. Chuck had been ill for some time with Parkinson's disease, but we had no idea that his last days were upon us. I was immediately hit with a shock of grief at the loss, as well as concern for my Mom. Chuck was the oldest of her siblings (Mom was the youngest) and he was the first sibling to pass away. For a brief moment I thought about coming back home, but I knew I was where I was supposed to be and that somehow, Chuck's passing was meant to be a part of my Camino experience. And so I began that day's walk with a heavy heart, deep in thought about life and death.

Early that morning I was walking down the path alone, when the path turned from dirt to stones, and they caught my attention. Two stones in particular called to me. If you've never had a stone call to you, trust me

– it happens. I just knew I was supposed to pick up these two stones, but I didn't know why. That awareness came a couple of days later.

A few days later I was taking a break, and I pulled out those two stones and held them in my hand. That's when it hit me – these two stones were for my Mom and for my cousin David (Uncle Chuck's oldest son). The Mom stone was a mix of brilliant white and dark gray, and it struck me that this represented my Mom's grief and losses. Since my brother Gregg's tragic death in 1980, Mom had carried around a heavy weight of grief – profound grief felt but rarely made known to others, covered up with smiles. Add to that the separation from my Dad and the loss of her marriage (and in many ways her identity), and Mom's life had been a grief journey for decades This stone spoke to me about grief – Mom's grief.

The David stone was also a brilliant white, but with a large dark area that seemed to overwhelm the white. I'd been thinking a lot about the mantle that David had been carrying and wearing for some time in taking care of his dad (Chuck) and in supporting his mom (Judy) through Chuck's illness and fading health. I kept thinking "what a weight that must be," and this stone – the David stone – spoke to me of that heavy mantle, a weight that it was time for David to put down and let go of. Now I knew what these stones were and what they represented, and I carried them in my pocket for the rest of my Camino journey until I arrived at the end of the world at Fisterra.

As if these stones hadn't already spoken enough to me about their purpose and meaning, they spoke to me one more time in a powerful way before I heaved them into the Atlantic Ocean. Several years before my Camino journey, my Mom had gifted me a necklace and pendant with a cross carved in it. I'm not a big fan of necklaces, but I decided to wear this precious gift from Mom from that day forward, and I wear it nearly every day now. Here's what was engraved on the back of the pendant:

My Dear Son,
May Gold always
Protect you and
Give you strength.

One more thing – there was a small diamond on the front of the pendant at the intersection of the cross.

Because the Camino journey was a wet one – from sweat and nearly daily rain – I took the necklace off early on my walk and, instead, carried it in my pocket (the same pocket as the stones). I didn't put on the pendant until after my Camino journey had ended, and that's when I realized that the diamond was gone, apparently knocked out by the two stones in my pocket.

The two letting go stones had caused the diamond to be lost, and my immediate response was to replace the diamond. But I never did, knowing that for some reason the diamond wasn't meant to be there and was, perhaps, another lesson in letting go and not being attached to things or outcomes. The pendant reminds me every day about letting go and that Mom is always watching over me. That pendant also now includes a charm gifted to me by my dear friend Jen Cabic, which includes my Mom's thumb print on one side and the words "Love Mom" in my Mom's signature on the other (with a butterfly as well). Always with me, Mom.

Many days later, when I arrived at Fisterra, I went about a ritual of the stones, starting with the stones given to me by two friends. I shot a short video of me at the end of the world and, without knowing what either of them had intended to let go of, I tossed the stones into the Atlantic Ocean. I also did the same with my two stones, heaving the stones off the end of the world and letting go of that which no longer served me. However, I was already aware that I'd let those thoughts, beliefs and relationships go while I was on my Camino journey.

Now it was time for the Mom stone and the David stone, and I again shot a brief video to share with David and Mom to let them know the story and symbolism of the stones. I sent the videos to my friends and to David once I returned, but I showed the video to Mom when I was with her on my first visit after returning from Spain. I told Mom the entire story and how the stone spoke to me about her grief, and I told her it was time to let go of the dark grief that she'd carried for so long. We shared a few tearful moments together, and my hope was and remains that the tossing of the Mom stone brought some small amount of release for Mom from her grief. All from just letting go!

What Are You Carrying?

We're all carrying things that don't serve us, at least not in a healthy way. Perhaps it's a belief about yourself, your worthiness or your enoughness.

We all carry around false beliefs and doubts about whether we're enough – smart enough, pretty enough, thin enough, successful enough, rich enough, lovable enough. Perhaps it's a loss you've suffered – a death, a broken or ended relationship, or a traumatic experience that has been a part of who you are for years or even decades. Perhaps it's a perspective you have about yourself, about how things work, about how relationships work, or about how the world works (e.g. I'm a failure, the world is dangerous and out to screw me, great relationships are a myth). Whatever it is that you're carrying (and likely have been carrying for a long time), it's keeping you from having the life experience and outcomes that you desire.

> Whatever it is that you're carrying (and likely have been carrying for a long time), it's keeping you from having the life experience and outcomes that you desire.

We often refer to these things we carry as baggage, and baggage goes far beyond relationships. There's life, money, business, employment, and every other conceivable kind of baggage, and they're all heavy. They all weigh us down. They can sometimes also be what we use to beat up other people in our lives. While there's a wide variety of types, weights and sources of the things that we carry, one thing is true for all of them – you have the ability to put them ALL down and to live life without them (or at least to continually lessen their weight and impact).

Before we further explore what you're carrying, let's get clear on one critical element about the things that you carry. Are you ready for this truth? You may not like it, and you'll most likely want to reject it. Here it is: the biggest obstacle to letting go is YOU. All of these things that we carry around didn't jump onto us and didn't attach themselves to us. Even if they were "gifted" to you by someone else, that person didn't and couldn't force you to carry it. We all choose what we carry, even if we know that carrying it is unhealthy and getting in the way of what we really want. Unless and until you're willing to accept that carrying something is *your choice*, you'll be unable to let it go because you're the one holding on to it.

Before you stop reading and conclude that I'm certifiable, stay with me for a bit longer as I explain. First, it just makes sense that we're all responsible for the choice to carry something. No matter what the nature or degree of our past experiences have been, neither experiences nor other people can force you to carry something. Yes, those experiences and people can metaphorically hand you a belief, a thought, or a perspective. They can even deliver a wound, but each one of us has the power to let it go because we made the choice – even if unconsciously – to carry it.

Second, acknowledging that you're choosing to carry something is an empowering awareness because if you can choose to carry it, *then you can choose to let it go*. It's the truth of the carrying choice that informs and proves the truth of your ability to let it go. This is perhaps the most empowering truth about the things you're carrying around that are getting in the way of the relationships and outcomes you so deeply desire. But you can't let anything go until you're fully aware of it, own that carrying it is your choice, get clear on the ways that carrying it is actually serving you, and choose to let that thing go and put it down – knowing that the process may be messy, uncomfortable and perhaps even painful.

Not only are you choosing to carry whatever it is that you're carrying, that carrying is also serving you in some way. In other words, you're getting something out of carrying it, even if you're aware of its extremely limiting and damaging impact. Here's another simple truth – we only do things that serve us in some way, even if we know that it's also having a negative impact. For example, in what ways could believing that you're not good enough serve you?

One obvious example is that if you believe you're not good enough, you'll play small and not take risks, which minimizes the risk of coming up short or failing. In other words, you avoid the risk of an outcome that might feed your belief that you're not good enough. In even clearer words, carrying your self-limiting beliefs and living life based upon those beliefs is a form of protection, and that protection is what serves you and allows you to rationalize (albeit mostly unconsciously) your ongoing carrying of that belief.

Let's look at another example. I have a coaching client who's conscious (now) that she's highly judgmental of other people. She's also now conscious that this judgmental nature is keeping her from forming the close relationships that she desires. Finally, she has become conscious that her judgmental nature and habit grew out of being negatively judged by her mother over the years, starting when she was young. So how does her self-limiting belief and judgmental behavior serve her? Simple – it keeps people at a distance so that they can't judge her and hurt her. Yes, they can and will still judge her, but this isn't obvious until you dig into her self-beliefs.

Until she realized that she was getting a "win" from her self-limiting beliefs and resulting judgmental behavior, it was nearly impossible for her to let it go and put it down because doing so would be perceived internally as being unsafe and at risk. While we're all and always at risk of rejection and being hurt, only when you become aware and conscious of the ways that your beliefs, perspectives and thinking are serving you can you begin to work on letting them go.

What beliefs or perspectives are you carrying? What hurt, loss or trauma are you choosing to carry around? What doubts about your worthiness or enoughness are you carrying around like an anchor and allowing to keep you from having what you really want in any part of your life? And most important, in what ways are these things that you're carrying serving you (likely protecting you), which creates a very real attachment to them and an unconscious aversion to letting them go? Is now the time for you to let go, and are you ready to take the risk that always comes with letting go?

Letting Go of Stories

In my personal leadership book *Unmask: Letting Go of Who You're "Supposed" to Be & Unleashing Your True Leader* (*Motivational Press 2014*), I shared a great deal about the concept of stories and story debunking. This all relates to the stories that we've created (or accepted) in our own heads about ourselves, about business, about relationships, about families and about the world. Everything that I just discussed ultimately comes down to some form of a story, and it's these stories that we can and must let go of (even in small bits at a time) in order to move towards and into our most authentic and empowered lives and experiences. I touched on some of this letting go process above, and here I want to offer you a simple formula or process to let go of whatever it is you want to let go of.

The Letting Go Formula consists of these five core elements:

1. Acknowledge that it's *you* that's holding on (so only you can let go)
2. Explore and understand what you're getting from holding on
3. Grieve the loss of whatever you're holding on to
4. Set a clear intention to let go
5. Allow it to slip away

Not only is it generally necessary that you address all five of these elements, but they typically unfold in order – acknowledge it, explore it, grieve it, set intention and let it slip away. You'll notice that I refer to what you're letting go of as "it," and that's intentional. I use this visual because we can only hold on to tangible objects, and the "it" reminds you that you're holding on to some *thing* (not to some *one*). It also supports the slipping away step, as you envision whatever it is slipping out of your grasp.

Acknowledge that You're the One Holding On

This may be a difficult step for many of you because we're all hesitant to recognize and then acknowledge that we're the one that's holding on to whatever it is that we want to let go of. That's one of the biggest hurdles to letting go because you can't let something go unless and until you admit that you're the one holding on. But if you're the one holding on, then you're in control of the letting go and you have the power to engage in the process of letting go. Too often, we're reluctant to take ownership of the holding on because (even if unconsciously) we're embracing our victimhood – choosing to think and believe that someone else or something else is doing something to us.

We also struggle in taking ownership of the holding on because it's far too easy for us to say to ourselves and others (and to actually believe) we don't want to continue experiencing whatever it is that we *want to let go of*. However, if you didn't want to continue the experience, you would have already let it go. Our conscious minds are quite powerful and can lead us to believe that because we *say we want to move on*, someone or something else must be *doing something to us* because we haven't been able to move on.

——— 🦋 ———

That's one of the biggest hurdles to letting go because you can't let something go unless and until you admit that you're the one holding on.

For example, think of a past relationship that's continuing to weigh on you. You say you've moved on, but you run into your prior partner (perhaps they're with a new partner), and you feel that lurch in your stomach that reminds you that you've not fully moved on. You say to yourself and others that you've moved on and that you're over the relationship, but there's something still lingering. It's far too easy to convince yourself that the past relationship *still has a hold of you*, but in reality it's YOU *that's still holding on to something about the past relationship*.

Forgiveness is a fantastic example of the letting go concept and the need to take ownership that you're the one holding on (and, in the case of forgiveness, the one who has to do the forgiving). Many years ago, a friend was sharing with me her desire that she "wished that her ex-husband would forgive her." When I heard this statement, I reacted by saying, "Why? That won't make any difference." She followed up (not surprisingly) by saying that his forgiveness was what she needed, and we then went through this brief exercise.

- **Me:** What does the lack of forgiveness feel like?
  - > Her: It feels like a sharp pain in my side.

- **Me:** How big is the pain?
  - > Her: It varies, but at times the pain is severe, and it's almost always there in some form.
- **Me:** Does it feel like a wound?
  - > Her: Yes, it feels like I was stabbed with a hook.
- **Me:** What size and kind of hook? A big hook, a small hook?
  - > Her: It's a giant hook, like the big gaffes they use for large fish.
- **Me:** Whose hook is it?
  - > Her: That's my point. It's his (ex-husband's) hook.
- **Me:** So, he gave it to you?
  - > Her: Yes, that's what I've been saying.
- **Me:** Who put it in you?
  - > Her: [Exhaling and slumping her shoulders] I did.
- **Me:** Yeah. He gave it to you, but you put it in and only you can take it out. He can't take it out because you put it in. This isn't about him forgiving you – this is about you forgiving yourself.

My guess is that reading the prior exchange hit home (and perhaps hard) for many of you, and this is the reality of forgiveness. The most important forgiveness for any of us is the act of truly forgiving ourselves.

There's an old saying that failing to forgive someone else is like drinking poison and hoping that the other person dies. When we choose not to forgive others, we're poisoning ourselves, and I'm sure that many of you have seen or personally experienced the ways that failing to forgive someone proves to be toxic for the person that's choosing not to forgive. Similarly, when you refuse to forgive yourself, you continue to ingest the poison of whatever judgments related to some prior actions, behaviors or choices. Much like the hook in the example above, some other person may continue to hand you the poison of judgment, but it's you who chooses to drink the poison. And you can only end this cycle when you choose to stop drinking the poison by forgiving yourself.

We want to believe that we've moved on and that other people or outside circumstances are continuing to haunt us. After all, who would *choose* to continue to experience something and carry it around? The answer is all of us because whatever you're carrying is something that you've chosen to carry, albeit nearly always unconsciously. Only if and when you acknowledge that you're choosing to carry it and hang on to it can you begin the process of letting it go.

What are you holding on to in your life? Perhaps it's a past relationship, a broken heart, mistrust or simply fear. Perhaps it's an old belief or story about the world, about other people or about yourself. Perhaps it's something you did in the past that you wish you hadn't done. Perhaps it's a judgment someone else had about you that you've somehow taken on as a self-judgment. Perhaps it's some deep sense of loss or grief from your life. Perhaps it's a mask (or masks) that you've been wearing to keep others from really seeing and knowing you. Indeed, only you can take off a mask and choose to let it slip out of your grasp.

No matter what it is that you're holding on to, the process of letting go *requires* that you first acknowledge that you are, indeed, holding on to it and that *only you can let it go.*

No matter what it is that you're holding on to, the process of letting go *requires* that you first acknowledge that you are, indeed, holding on to it and that *only you can let it go.* Stop waiting for something or for some feeling to go away (it never will), and instead take the courageous step to accept personal responsibility for the holding on. While this step may be challenging, it's an empowering first step and one through which you'll experience a great sense of control, knowing that you're the one that holds the key to letting go.

Understanding What You're Getting from Holding On

As challenging as the first step (acknowledgement) is, this second step is often even more difficult. Despite its logic and simplicity, it can feel so counterintuitive to believe that you want to hold on to something that you say you want to move on from. That's the tricky part because your mind tells you that if you want to move on, then there must be nothing good in what you want to move on from. But that's the lie – because we only do things that give us something in return, *even if that return is somewhat or completely unhealthy.* I call this exploring and looking for the win you're getting from holding on. After all, if you're getting a win from holding on, you can't possibly let go unless and until you understand and acknowledge what that win is and get clear that you're ready to let go of that win.

Let's take a little deeper look at the logic that proves the truth that we hold on because of what we're getting (not because we can't let go). If there's something that you want to move on from, stop doing or let go of, one possibility is that you're struggling to move on or let go because you just can't do it. That makes no sense unless you want to play the victim and claim that it's some form of *shit happens.* In contrast, consider the premise that if you're struggling to move on or let go of something or someone, it's because you're getting something for yourself out of not letting go. Here's the tricky part – in many cases, what you're getting is some form of reinforcement of an unhealthy belief about yourself.

For example, most of us at some time and in some way engage in beating ourselves up. Why do we beat ourselves up? Simple: because we believe that we deserve to be beat up, and it might as well be by ourselves. Why do we play small? Simple again, because if we play small our risks are limited to small failures, but if we play big (whatever that means to you) then we increase the risk of a big failure. Why are we hesitant to be vulnerable and authentic? Because we're afraid that people will see who we really are, and *we have doubts about whether the real us is worthy.*

It feels safer to be judged on who we pretend to be than to be judged on who we really are, so we hold tight to our masks and regularly hide behind them. We're all incredibly powerful beings, and we certainly have the power to make different choices, including moving on and letting go. Our failures to let go aren't because we don't want to let go bad enough – it's because we're getting something at some level that serves us by holding on.

Think about some behavior that you continue to engage in, even if it's clear that it's not good for you. Not only are others telling you that it's not good for you, but you know it for yourself. Let's look at some simple examples. Most people would acknowledge that smoking cigarettes isn't good for their health, yet many people struggle to quit smoking. Certainly, there are some physical elements in the form of the addiction to nicotine. However, most smokers who admit the unhealthy nature of smoking know that they get something from smoking. Perhaps it's a form of relaxation. Perhaps it's a sense of belonging. Whatever the source, one of the biggest challenges of quitting smoking is what you get from it (beyond the nicotine impact).

Relationships are a great example of this reality. I know many people who continue to have strong feelings for someone from a past relationship, even if they know the relationship was unhealthy and even if they're adamant that they're grateful to have moved on. You never know the source of great wisdom, but I recently experienced it from an episode of *Dexter* (the Showtime series). The situation was as extreme as you can get – a woman (Debra) who had dated and fallen in love with a serial killer – yet she seemed to be missing him. Another woman (Rita) was struggling with moving on from an abusive relationship, and she commented that she missed the parts of her ex-husband that were real and good. Debra's comment was profound and went something like this: "*We don't miss what was real. We miss how he made us feel about ourselves.*"

Herein lies a trap – how they felt about themselves is *real* – it's true about them – but it's not a consistent self-belief for them. These men (and this is true in many real-life relationships) did help Debra and Rita feel good about themselves, so it was natural for them to continue to hold on to the past relationships and feelings in some way because it was their connection to feeling a certain way about themselves.

This process – exploring and understanding what you get out of holding on – can be extremely difficult, especially when exploring it on your own. This is the land of blind spots, and it often requires someone else to ask you questions to help you uncover and discover the win (or wins) you're getting from holding on. Your unconscious is often more powerful than your conscious mind, especially as you're beginning the journey to greater awareness. Even as you move more thoughts and beliefs from your unconscious to your conscious, your unconscious will always be a source of blind spots and hidden beliefs. It's too easy for you (and me) on our own to avoid the truth of what we're getting from holding on. A great start is to acknowledge that there must be some win you're getting from holding on. You can then start exploring and uncovering (because it may be buried), committed to not giving up until you find the deepest and truest win for you in holding on. Even when you find a win, it may not be the win that's the source of your holding on behavior, which is another reason to seek support from others to walk with you through this journey of self-awareness and truth telling.

The great part of this process of exploring and understanding the true reasons you're holding on (what you're getting from it) is that once you uncover and own them, you'll feel your grip relaxing on whatever it is

The great part of this process of exploring and understanding the true reasons you're holding on (what you're getting from it) is that once you uncover and own them, you'll feel your grip relaxing on whatever it is you're holding on to.

you're holding on to. The process of letting go is still not complete, but this important step will do the most to prepare you to let go. After all, you can't let go of something that you want to hold on to unless and until you confront your reasons for holding on and make a new conscious decision to begin the process of letting go. Essentially, you're choosing to move towards what you get from letting go because it's more important to you than what you're getting from holding on.

Before moving on to the next step in the letting go process, I want to spend a few minutes focusing on one of the most difficult things for many of us to let go of – outcomes. We want to believe (and often do believe) that we control outcomes, and control is often at the heart of the challenges we're facing with letting go. In fact, the very act of holding on is an act of control, but the sooner you can admit that you don't control outcomes (that you can only influence them), the faster you can claim and tap into your true power. For only when you give up the control that you think you have can you unleash the power that you truly have in the forms of authenticity and choices.

While you want to control outcomes and results, what you really control is yourself. Yes, there are always challenges with lack of awareness and unconscious thoughts tripping you up, but you can commit to and work on being more aware and bringing your unconscious thoughts into your conscious thinking. I can personally attest to the truth that when I let go of my false sense that I control other people, situations and outcomes, and instead devote all of my energy to the one person that I do control (me), I experience levels of peace, joy and presence that are transformative. I'll talk more about this topic in Chapter 15 (Just Be Present), but for now remember that you don't control other people, situations or outcomes.

The other key point relative to letting go of the false sense of control is the unhealthy and unfulfilling attachment we have to outcomes – more specifically, the ways that we attach our own sense of self-worth and value to our outcomes. For most of us, not achieving the outcome that we desired isn't what frustrates and disappoints us – rather, it's what we make the outcome mean about us. It's all too typical for us to attach our sense of self-worth to whatever outcome we get, for better or for worse. If I want to get a raise and don't get it, I can start to think that I'm not worthy of the raise (or just generally not worthy), despite that fact that I only had the ability to influence the raise through my words, actions and efforts. The fact that someone else decided not to give me a raise doesn't mean that I'm less worthy or not worthy.

The same is true in relationships. Yes, there are times that your relationship partner decides to end the relationship (and you may not want the relationship to end), but too often we attach self-worth and meaning to the other person's choice, which we don't control. Yes, it's important for me to take a close look at the ways that I showed up (or didn't show up) in the relationship, but the other person's decision to end it (or my own decision to end it for my own reasons, for that matter) doesn't make me less than or unworthy.

Similarly, I don't follow the mantra of setting low expectations to avoid or minimize being disappointed. That approach doesn't serve me or my mission. Instead, I believe in setting high expectations for myself and the outcomes I desire, while at the same time not personally attaching my worth or value to the outcomes of those desires and expectations. The problem isn't with setting expectations too high, but rather with too high a level of personal attachment to the outcomes. Certainly, I want to assess what I did and thought (or didn't do or didn't think) relative to the outcomes I was pursuing, and my own self-worth beliefs may have been a factor in what I did or didn't do, BUT by detaching from the outcomes I can play big and be bold, focus on myself and let the outcomes unfold.

As you assess yourself relative to the things that you're holding on to, make sure to consider the ways and degree to which you're holding on to and attaching yourself (and your self-worth) to the outcomes. My guess is that many of you reading this book have some work to do around attachment to outcomes through this letting go process. Just remember that the process of letting go is an insider job and that you are (and always have been) in full and nearly complete control of the only person who matters when it comes to letting go – YOU!

Grieve the Loss

No matter how unhealthy a situation or relationship was, and no matter how negative your feelings are regarding a person, a relationship, a situation or an outcome, there's nearly always something good in it that needs to be grieved when you let it go. There are situations and experiences in our lives that cause pain – sometimes the pain is in the situation or experience itself, sometimes the pain is from the loss of something or someone, and most often there's a combination of both. Too often, and for what can seem like good reasons, we seek to move on (to let go) before we've grieved the loss of the good parts of what was. While it can feel good to say, "I've moved on," too often we haven't moved on but rather just put away or compartmentalized what we want to say we've moved on from.

Many people claim to be great at compartmentalizing, but I don't buy it, and I don't know anyone who has developed a leak-proof heart compartment. Even if you feel you can compartmentalize, I don't believe that this is healthy. In fact, think about what compartmentalization is – the act of putting something in a compartment. It's not at all the same as the act of removing something or, even healthier, moving on and letting go in a good way.

Think about some food that has rotted on the kitchen counter and has started to smell. You can put it in the trash can in the kitchen, which reduces the smell, but the food is still rotten and the smell is still there. You can then move the trash bag to the bins in the garage, but the food is still rotten and the smell is still there – you simply moved it so you didn't have to experience it so much. However, the rotten food and the smell only go away when you remove it completely (that is, when they come to take the garbage). Until it's gone, in fact, the smell often lingers.

The same is true of past experiences that we've compartmentalized. I'm not denying that you can compartmentalize things, but I'm rejecting the idea that doing so removes the problem. Whatever impact the past experience had continues to exist and even rot, but it only does so inside of you where others can't see it (or so you think). So many times in my life I've heard people say that they've compartmentalized something and suggested that therefore they've moved on, but it's obvious to everyone else that they haven't moved on or let go. I know that you've seen it in others around you as well, and likely even with yourself.

We all know that grief is a process that has various stages, and those stages are real. While the stages and timing of the stages may vary for everyone, it's important that you embrace the reality of grief whenever you're looking to move on from something. Admittedly, grief may not ever fully leave us. My good friend Bob Gribble has shared this with me over the years: "You can only grieve that which you loved." In this form, grief is about love and per-haps some element of the grief will never leave us, but there's still a reality that we can't release that which we have not yet grieved. Therefore,

Grief is about love and perhaps some element of the grief will never leave us, but there's still a reality that we can't release that which we have not yet grieved.

allowing yourself to grieve is a critical step in the letting go process.

Make sure to look for the loss to be grieved whenever you're looking to move on and let go of something. Even if the circumstances are so difficult that you can't imagine there being anything to grieve, look for and find that which you need to grieve. Otherwise, you'll be seeking to let go of something (or some part of something) that you've not yet grieved, and that lack of grieving is akin to trying to let go of something while still having it tied to one of your fingers. It can't happen.

As for my Mom, I don't think she ever really allowed herself to grieve my brother Gregg's death. To my knowledge, she never sought professional help other than her minister and conversations with friends, and I don't know if she ever really talked about her pain. I know that Mom lived with grief for the rest of her life after Gregg's death – grief beyond the loss of someone she loved – and that grief ate her alive. For much of her life, she lived with depression that few people ever knew, because she kept it hidden behind a big smile and a helping heart. Later in life, she also suffered a deep loss when her marriage to my Dad ended – yet another deep loss that I don't believe she ever grieved, and which also ate her up on the inside.

Mom would tell me that she'd moved on from these losses, but I don't believe it, in part because she never acknowledged how much she was holding on to the loss and the anger, and in part because she never really grieved the losses. She was holding on so tight to the darkness of her grief that she couldn't really experience joy. I'm sad that this was Mom's journey, and I hope that the small act of letting go that I did for her in Spain gave her some comfort in the last year of her life.

What are you holding on to and continuing to experience in your life that's not serving you? Have you identified the loss and the grief that goes with it, whether for all of it or parts of it? Have you acknowledged the grief and allowed yourself to process and move through it? Even if the past experience is painful and seems to have nothing in it that you would want to grieve, take a closer look. There's nearly always something that's lost from even the most hurtful experience, and whatever has been lost must be grieved before you move on and before you let go.

Set a Clear Intention to Let Go

Once you've acknowledged your ownership of the holding on, uncovered the reasons that you're holding on, and grieved whatever has been lost, the final stages of letting go are just around the corner. Indeed, the first three steps in the letting go formula are usually the most challenging. You see, the first three steps are all ways that you actually hold on – reasons that you're unable or unwilling to let go – so dealing with these steps leaves a clear path to letting go as you set a clear intention to do so. If you want to change a behavior or way of thinking, you'll need to be intentional (the constant mindset of setting an intention), and being intentional requires being crystal clear with the first three steps in the letting go process.

I believe in the power of words, and setting an intention is a great example. Consider the differences between the following:

> I'll try to let it go.
> I want to let it go.
> I hope to let it go.
> I have to let it go.
> I need to let it go.
> *I intend to let it go.*

The final step after intention is *I'm letting go*, which happens in Step Five below. While setting the intention doesn't ensure that you let go – you still have to actually let go – the act of setting a clear intention is like drawing a line in the sand, and it also wires your conscious and unconscious thoughts towards letting go.

Once you've consciously set your intention towards letting go, with clarity on the first three steps discussed above, it's as if you've wired your thinking (conscious and unconscious), beliefs and actions towards letting go. And then the letting go process (it's still a process, as discussed in Step Five below) will unfold almost unconsciously, as if it were programmed into your psyche. Indeed, setting a clear intention is a form of programming your thinking and actions towards letting go.

While intention setting is often easier than the first three steps, there's a key element to intention setting that might be in your way. It can sometimes come up in Step Two (understanding the reasons that you're holding on), but whenever it comes up it flows from and through our own self-worth beliefs. To be clear, we don't have to fully believe in our own self-worth (there may always be doubts), but many times we can only let go to the degree we believe ourselves to be worthy of letting go. In other words, many times our holding on behavior is driven by questions and uncertainty about our self-worth (our enoughness), and we hold on *because* we don't believe we're worthy. Think of it this way – we hold on to old experiences, old beliefs, old stories and old hurts because we're not worthy and confident enough to move on and leave the past in the past.

The process of setting clear intentions is different for different people, and there's no required way of doing it. Certainly, it's important to set clear intentions and to be intentional (pun intended) with the words you use in setting the intention (see above). It's also often helpful to clearly articulate what you learned and uncovered in the first three steps. One way to do this is to journal about your letting go process, experience and journey to help make sure that you've seen and learned all that you can through the process. The act of writing it down can make it more real and open your eyes to even more insights and new perspectives – perspectives that can help ensure an effective letting go process. This intention setting process may also involve declaring and using affirmations, which will help to address any lingering self-worth obstacles to the process of letting go.

When you set intentions you're declaring who you are, cutting the connection (often unhealthy) that you had with past experiences, beliefs and actions.

When you set intentions you're declaring who you are, cutting the connection (often unhealthy) that you had with past experiences, beliefs and actions, and claiming a new way of living and being without whatever it is that you've been holding on to. No matter which specific process you use for setting clear intentions, just make sure to be clear and committed. From here there's only one thing to do – *to let it gently slip away from your grasp.*

Allow It to Slip Away

This fifth and final step is less a step and more like an awareness – an awareness that the process of letting go (and the ultimate act of letting go) usually isn't a single moment, event or occurrence. It's typically not accompanied by a lightning bolt or an in the moment awareness that you've let go. Rather, you go through many purposeful and intentional steps and processes to let go, never certain if you've really let it go. And then one day you "look down" at your hands and you realize that you're no longer holding it (whatever it was), because it has slipped away over time.

Part of this awareness involves being gentle with yourself and being patient, not expecting that you'll waive some type of magic wand and whatever you've been holding will be gone. Letting go usually doesn't work this way. Rather than being a single act of letting go, it's a process (as described above) that results in you releasing your grip, cutting the things and beliefs that were tethering it to you, and then letting the intention setting process work its magic towards letting go.

So how will you know when you've really let it go? You generally will not know when it actually happens, and there typically isn't even a moment of letting go. You'll know that you've let it go when a situation arises and you no longer feel that tug or twist that you felt in the past. I've been asked how I knew that I'd let go of the hurt of a past relationship, and the answer was easy – when I saw pictures of my past partner on Facebook with her new love and I didn't feel anything I used to feel. I didn't feel loss, pain or sadness. I didn't feel any tug in my stomach. I didn't feel any regret or thoughts of what might have been. I only felt unconditional love for her and a sincere desire that she (and her new partner) live a life filled with love and joy. My only thought was to bless her and them, without any thought or feeling (conscious or unconscious) of what it meant for or about me. Don't expect to know *when* you let it go, but you'll most certainly know when *it's gone*.

Remember this important point – when you let go of anything or anyone, it's an act of releasing something or someone that's holding you back, slowing you down or even tethering you. Just imagine the relief and lightness you'll feel when you've let go of whatever it is that you're holding on to. In some cases, what you hold on to feels like a rope or tether. In other cases, who you hold on to may feel like a burden or a weight. No matter what the feeling is like for you, letting something or someone go is an act of release, and it frees you up. Yes, freedom is the outcome of letting go, a freedom that opens you and your life up to more love, more passion, more connection, more influence and more impact. The question isn't whether you can let go, but whether you're willing to do the challenging work (and it is work) to move you from your holding on place to your letting go place, and then to your freedom place.

What are you holding on to in your life? Are you prepared to do the work – the sometimes-painful work involved in letting go? Are you willing to be vulnerable and honest with yourself, and to ask others around you to do the same with you? Are you willing to take personal ownership of your acts of holding on and to thereby empower yourself to move through the letting go process? Most important of all, are you willing to believe in yourself enough to let go? If your answers to these questions are clear, then I invite you to begin the journey toward letting go with the most important first step – admitting that you're the one who's holding on! If you're ready to let go – it all begins with *Just One Step*!

Chapter 9

Just Explore

*H*ave you ever been lost? Have you ever felt lost? I'm sure that I have at some point in my life (at least metaphorically), but one specific experience on the Camino taught me this powerful lesson about life and choices – Lost Is a Choice! While there are many elements to this life truth, the two most important elements are trust and a surrender to the adventure that life is (and is meant to be). While the entire Camino journey was indeed intended to be an adventure, I learned this lesson about being lost and having a choice on my final day on the Camino.

My original plan (I'm laughing out loud as I write the word plan when it comes to the Camino) was to travel from Villafranca del Bierzo to Santiago de Compostela (the official finish of the Camino), and then to travel to the end of the world (Fisterra). The walk from Santiago to Fisterra is approximately 55 miles. From Fisterra, I'd planned to then walk to the other Camino city on the Atlantic (Muxia, 20 miles) to finish my journey. However, those plans changed on the second day after I left Santiago. I'd walked fifteen miles to the village of Logoso, where I'd planned (or more accurately, hoped) to spend the night. However, once again there was no room at the inn, and I was left with two choices.

First, I could continue as planned towards Fisterra and likely find a place to stay after walking another ten miles on already pained feet and aching legs. Second, I could change my plan and instead head in the direction of Muxia, and I was assured that there'd be a place to sleep in the village of Dumbria, only four miles away on that route. I quickly decided to head for Muxia, and I did find a place to sleep that night. The next day I arrived in the beautiful oceanside city of Muxia, where I enjoyed a wonderful dinner, evening and cigar overlooking the Atlantic Ocean.

The next morning, I set out for Fisterra (now the final leg of my Camino journey), which would involve a twenty-mile walk over the course of approximately eight hours. It was a beautiful morning with plenty of sunshine, and I set out heading southwest towards Fisterra. For the first half hour that morning, I was making my way along the Camino trail; however, the trail from Muxia to Fisterra isn't well marked (apparently, many fewer people walk this way). To put it simply, early that morning I lost the Camino trail, and I walked four and a half hours that day wandering through northern Spain without being on the Camino. I knew the general direction from Muxia to Fisterra (southwest), so I kept walking and trusting.

My wanderings took me down roads, trails and paths. I walked through small villages and across fields, and I spent much of that morning walking through dense forests. There were roads (dirt roads), but no signs for miles and miles. One interesting element of my walk that morning is that during the entire four and a half hours I saw only one person and not one vehicle. I saw some animals (dogs, cats, chickens, cows and birds), but no people. It was the epitome of being alone and literally lost in the woods, but what I realized then and now is that I was never really lost, and I never felt lost. This was the beginning of the lesson that lost is a choice.

Many years ago, my nephew Blake (my brother's son) was heavily involved with robotics competitions, and he (along with his family and the robotics team) was in Indianapolis for a large competition with thousands of people in attendance. During the competition, Blake went missing, and my brother and his wife were frantically looking for him. They had security looking for Blake, but they couldn't find him. After approximately thirty minutes (which seemed like hours), my sister-in-law Becky found Blake sitting in the one of the rooms watching the competitions. Becky was relieved and crying, and so grateful to find Blake. When Blake asked why she was crying, Becky said that she was scared because he'd been lost and they couldn't find him. Blake's response was profound: "I wasn't lost. I knew where I was the whole time." WOW. Drop the microphone, Blake – you nailed it. He knew where he was the whole time, and *lost is a choice*.

When I was making my way from Muxia to Fisterra, I wasn't on the Camino and I didn't know exactly which way I was going, only where I was headed. All I knew was that I was in northern Spain and somewhere near the Camino, and

> "I wasn't lost. I knew where I was the whole time."

that was enough for me to keep walking, to keep wandering and to keep choosing. I had to make many choices that morning, with very little information to make those choices. While I had a pretty good idea of which direction was southwest, my choices at road and trail intersections or splits were often unclear in terms of direction, and there were no signs to guide me. I had to make choices based upon instincts and guesses, and I kept walking. In case you're wondering, I had GPS on my phone, but I was not about to use it – that was not the point of this adventure.

At some point, I realized that I had to get off of the roads because, while they might eventually get me to Fisterra, they would likely make the journey much longer. Remember, roads are made for cars and therefore often without regard to the shortest distance. I needed to find a more direct walk to Fisterra, so I intuitively decided that I'd take the next left when I found a trail and get off the road. I soon came upon my first left and took that trail down between farm fields, and that's when the weather changed. The early morning sun had turned to clouds, and within two hundred yards of turning onto this new trail, it started to rain (hard). Oh well, time for the poncho again.

After walking another three hundred yards, my new trail … ended. So much for those instincts. But there was a trail, sort of, and I began to make my way down what used to be a trail, which was largely overgrown with tall grass and prickly bushes. Did I mention that I was wearing shorts? So, I beat my way through and down this trail using my walking sticks and getting cut up along the way, and then I quickly came to the end of the former trail as well. It was a dead end. To my left was woods, and behind me was the way I'd come, and I wasn't going back. I had talked with Mark about this at dinner the night before I began my Camino journey, and he'd shared his personal philosophy to never backtrack. I'd chosen the same philosophy, so that left what was to my right – a large, open farm field – and I took it.

Poet Robert Frost famously and prophetically wrote these words in "The Road Not Taken":

Two roads diverged in a yellow wood,
And sorry I could not travel both
And be one traveler, long I stood
And looked down one as far as I could
To where it bent in the undergrowth;

Then took the other, as just as fair,
And having perhaps the better claim,
Because it was grassy and wanted wear;
Though as for that, the passing there
Had worn them really about the same,

And both that morning equally lay
In leaves no step had trodden black.
Oh, I kept the first for another day!
Yet knowing how way leads on to way,
I doubted if I should ever come back.

I shall be telling this with a sigh
Somewhere ages and ages hence:
Two roads diverged in a wood, and I—
I took the one less traveled by,
And that has made all the difference.

I was, indeed, living and walking the experience that Robert Frost described. I was taking the road less traveled, which has been a big part of my life experience for the past twenty years. And now the road less traveled adventure was becoming literally and metaphorically more pronounced and profound, here in northern Spain.

When I'd crossed the field, I found another path and took a left (sensing that this was more or less south in direction), but I soon found myself at a crossroads. The path had ended at a small road, and my choices were left or right. Since Fisterra was to the west, I chose to go right, which I was guessing was mostly westerly in direction. Once I again I listened to my intuition, which told me to take the next left (whatever it was or looked like). I guess it was a form of commitment and represented trusting myself. I soon found a trail (again, sort of) to my left and, while it wasn't much of a trail, I took it – following my intuitive commitment. Within two hundred yards, a much nicer path crossed and I took that to the left again, still trusting. After just one hundred yards of walking, I found what I was looking for – a Camino signpost. I'd found it – I'd found the Camino. I'd wandered, not knowing where I was, trusting myself and trusting that I was and would be okay.

In that moment of discovery, standing in the rain on the Camino in northern Spain, I did something that I hadn't yet done on the Camino – I danced. My face lit up, and I danced a jig on the Camino. Many have guessed that I was dancing because I was no longer lost, but they're wrong. I'd never been lost, and I've had to clarify this hundreds of times since my Camino journey. I was never lost, and I never felt lost. Yes, I lost the Camino and didn't know where I was (other than northern Spain), but I was simply taking a detour on my Camino adventure.

Have you guessed it? Why I was dancing? Because I'd had an adventure. My little boy inside was dancing because he'd just experienced a walk down the road, through the woods, over the hills, through the towns, not knowing exactly where he was going, but just having the adventure. And in the grand expanse of this part of Spain, I'd found the Camino, and I was back on the trail to my destination. It wasn't perfect or straight. It had many twists and turns – and setbacks. It had some admitted moments of uncertainty (which way do I go?). I was hungry and thirsty (a lesson learned about making sure to have more water).

I was many things (including wet, cold and tired), but one thing I wasn't and hadn't been all day was lost. I was rejoicing through dance not because I was no longer lost, but because I'd just experienced an amazing adventure. On the road as in life, I'd embraced the adventure and the uncertainty and found my way. I'd taken the road less traveled and, as Robert Frost inspired us, "that made all the difference." I'd experienced and embraced the adventure on the Camino, and we all have the choice to similarly embrace the adventure in our lives – a pivotal choice for all of us.

There's No Stuck

There have been times in my life (in the past) when I felt lost and said so, whether it was meant generally or specifically about a certain aspect of my life, and this is something I regularly hear from others. However, I now realize that lost isn't a truth, but rather a choice. No matter what's

I now realize that lost isn't a truth, but rather a choice.

happening in my life (or not happening the way I desire), I now realize that the idea of being lost or stuck isn't real. In short, there's no lost and there's no stuck. Yes, there are times of uncertainty, doubt and fear, but lost and stuck are decisions that we make. They're not outcomes, and they certainly aren't states of being that anyone else or anything else can inflict on you. No matter how alone you may be or feel (and there's a big difference), you always have a choice as to whether you stay alone, feel lost or decide to be stuck. These are choices you make at your core, and your choices will determine the nature and outcomes of your life's adventure.

When I was wandering around northern Spain, and especially in the woods where I was facing a choice of trails without any outside guidance of which way to go, I had four choices: take the left fork, take the right fork, go back or stand still (and wait and hope for someone else to find me). I'm sure that every one of you is saying that standing still isn't really a good choice, but how many times in your life have you done (or are you doing) precisely that – choosing to stand still and not make a choice, waiting for someone else, something else or other outside circumstances to make the decision for you?

You want to believe that this choice (standing still) is the safest because you think you can't be wrong if you don't decide. There's some truth in this thinking – yes, you can blame other people and circumstances for whatever happens or doesn't happen – but this is the choice of the victim and the blamer. We also forget this wisdom from the song "Freewill" by Rush: "If you choose not to decide, you still have made a choice." And it's rarely the right one.

When you're feeling stuck, what you're really saying is one or more of the following:

I don't know the right answer or direction, and I'm afraid to choose.

I don't the right answer or direction, and I don't want to be responsible if I choose badly.

I don't know the right answer or direction, and I'm choosing to stay here and let other people or circumstances decide for me.

I don't know the right answer or direction, and I don't trust myself to choose.

What are the essential elements of all of these? There are four: fear, protection, victimhood and lack of trust. It's important to address all of these directly in order to get unstuck, to move forward and to get unlost.

In order to address the foregoing obstacles, there are a couple of first steps. First, you have to pause, but remember that pausing isn't the same as stopping or being stuck. However, you must use discernment to make sure that your pausing has not turned into stopping and choosing stuck. I've had times in my life when I was in continuous motion, but the motion and action had no direction. In fact, the motion itself was a reaction to my fear and was a form of avoiding decisions and understanding. It was a way to protect myself (or so I thought), including protecting myself from being honest with myself or others. I was afraid that if I stopped, I'd be acknowledging my stuckness or lostness, and I didn't want anyone to know I was feeling lost, so I kept moving for appearance. Constant movement and action was and is also a great form of victimhood – if I keep moving at 100 miles per hour, I can always tell myself and others that I'm super busy and doing a lot, so if things don't turn out the way I hope or plan, then I can blame the world for not delivering.

Does any of this sound familiar for you? Are you hiding behind lots of motion and activity? Are you always busy, but not sure where you're going or even intending to go? Are you living the adventure, or are you hiding behind lots of activity? Are you doing many things because you're uncertain as to what to do and afraid to claim and commit to a path? Do you take time to pause, assess and understand? In most cases, part of your adventure requires that you slow down and even pause, because only in the pause can you ask yourself the questions that need to be answered for you to move forward. The pause is essential for you to ask and answer the questions above when it comes to feeling stuck or lost. The pause is where and when you better understand yourself and are able to make the choices that serve you, to consciously embrace the adventure of life, and to choose your direction wisely. Never lost, never stuck, only pausing!

The second critical step along with the pause is one we've talked about before – asking yourself the difficult questions *and honestly answering them.* One of the most difficult questions to ask and answer is about your fears. We all have fears, even if they're mostly unconscious. We falsely think that if we don't feel afraid (i.e. flight or fight response), then we're not afraid and fear isn't a factor in our situation. However, most of the fears holding us back are not conscious – they're unconscious fears that are running the show behind the scenes and in the shadows. And it's fear that feeds the lost or stuck story in our heads.

Much like the great and powerful Oz, pulling the levers behind the curtain, our unconscious fears slow us, trip us and stop us, often without us realizing it. Even when we're merely hesitating with our progress or taking longer than we had expected or hoped to make a decision, to put a decision into action or to reach our desired outcome, fear is the likely culprit or at least a contributing factor. Let's face it – fear exists to keep us safe, and being safe is a natural state of mind and desire. The only question is how safe you want to be – and whether the things that are important to you are important enough to move you past and through your fears even when that feels unsafe.

Think about indecision – we've all been there, and perhaps you're there right now. We say we're not being indecisive (we don't want to admit to this) – that we're just trying to figure out the best answer or the right answer. Hello? Hello! This is the fear talking. Yes, it's important to invest some time in gathering facts, analyzing different scenarios and making risk assessments, but there comes a time when we must make a decision and take action (or no action) based upon that decision.

What's procrastination? Fear in action. What's analysis paralysis? Fear in action. What's indecision? Fear in action. What's the unending search for the best or right answer? Fear in action. Only when you're willing to embrace the reality of fear, and bring it out of the shadows into consciousness, can you take back the control that fear can have over all of us. When you bring the fear into the light, it has little or no control over you, and you can then make decisions based upon all the required factors (other than fear). This doesn't mean that you proceed without fear, but that you make decisions and proceed *with an assessment of the fear.*

This doesn't mean that you proceed without fear, but that you make decisions and proceed *with an assessment of the fear.*

The Reality of Fear

As we'll discuss in Chapter 15 (Just Be Present), when you're truly present you won't experience fear (conscious or unconscious), since fear can't exist when you're in the present. Yes, the fear exists in the present (you feel the fear in the moment), but only when you're unwilling or unable to be in the present. When you're present, you're not looking into the future and anticipating possible negative outcomes (the source of fear). It's naïve, however, to believe that you can always be in the present so that you never experience fear. The question is not whether you experience fear, but how quickly you recognize it and move through it.

In addition, there's a process you can use to assess your fears. First, go looking for the fear and assume that fear is playing some role in whatever you're facing, whether it be indecision, stuckness, lostness, uncertainty, doubt or procrastination. If you don't assume fear's existence and impact, then you'll likely convince yourself that you're not afraid and thus miss the key factor that will help you to move forward by bringing your fears into the light.

Second, honestly assess the fears. What are they? Go deep with this question. For example, if you say that you're afraid of failing, go deeper into the question by asking *why* you're afraid of failing. We all fail, we all know it, and it's easy to believe that we have a fear of failing. However, we all have *different* fears of failure. For some, it's a fear of the judgment of others – not that you failed, but that you're a failure. For others, it's a fear that if you fail you'll lose people in your life. In fact, your deeper fear might not be the loss of people, but the ultimate fear of being alone. For others, it's the fear that a failure will feed their already existing "not enough" story (that they're a failure, that they're worthless, etc.). We avoid failing for fear that our psyche can't take another failure that will confirm the not good enough story inside us. Keep going with your questions about what you're afraid of so that you truly understand the fear and its depth. Only then can you take the next step in assessing and moving through your fears.

Third, ask yourself about the likelihood of that which you truly fear. Start with the superficial fear (e.g. failure, making a mistake, looking bad) and carefully assess how likely each of the feared outcomes is. You'll nearly always discover that the likelihood of the feared outcomes is pretty low, and this alone can help to release some of fear's hold on you. Then go to the deeper fear questions, and in doing so you'll discover two things. First, you'll see that the likelihood of these deeper fears becoming a reality is extremely low or even minute. Second, you'll discover that your fears are largely unfounded and that you're more committed to your desired future than to protecting yourself by allowing the fear to hold you back. For example, when you face the truth that you have a fear of being exposed as a fraud because of your own self-worth issues, you'll discover that the fear is less about others and more about yourself. Once you realize that your own insecurities are the sources of your fears and hesitations, you'll often find that you'll own more of your own power through the confidence that you're enough. Your own not enough stories can keep you stuck *because they're unconscious,* and when you bring them out of the shadows into your conscious you disempower them and empower yourself.

Fourth, ask yourself what you control and what you don't control about the situation, challenge or opportunity where you feel afraid. You'll certainly find that you control very little (in fact, only yourself) and that most everything is outside of your control. Initially, this is a difficult truth to accept, but ultimately it will empower you with the reality that you have control over everything that matters – YOU. Yes, you have the ability to influence other people and situations; however, that influence comes from your choices and the ways you show up (or don't show) up with other people and in those situations. It all comes back to you. While you may not like this truth in the beginning (no more blaming here), it will bring you to being laser focused on the only person that matters – YOU. Now, you can focus your time, attention and energy on what you'll do (or not do), what you'll commit to (or say no to), which direction you'll head and the many ways that you can show up for yourself and influence and impact others. This process of assessing control (or more accurately lack of control) is an important part of navigating through and past any fears you might have.

Finally, we come down to action. There's an old proverb that goes like this:

Question: There are three birds sitting on a fence, and one decides to fly away. How many birds are still sitting on the fence?
Answer: Three. Deciding to fly away isn't the same as flying away.

Action is what takes all of your thinking, assessment and discernment and makes it a reality. Action is what puts the wheels of change into motion. Action is required to change your current reality. Yes, sometimes that action might be to do nothing (or to say no), but even a decision to do nothing is a decision (and an action). The question is whether you're choosing not to do something (a conscious choice) or defaulting into no action (indecision). No matter how good your assessments may be, they must be followed by conscious action in order to move forward, and especially to move beyond feeling stuck and lost. I'd made all sorts of assessments and discernments in the woods in Spain, but I'd still be sitting there if I hadn't made the choice to choose a direction and to keep walking – always one step at a time.

What Do You Trust

Even after you've fully and deeply assessed the fears at play and gotten your fears out in front of you, taking action will always require some degree of trust. Because there are no guarantees or absolutes, there will always be uncertainties. It's in this realm of uncertainty where trust is required, and there are various forms of trust. In communication and relationships, we often talk about trust in terms of trusting other people, but in this context, the two trust questions aren't about other people. The questions are about whether (and to what degree) you trust yourself and whether (and to what degree) you trust that things will work out and be okay (and that you'll be okay). It's these two elements of trust that will serve you most in your adventure of life.

Even after you've fully and deeply assessed the fears at play and gotten your fears out in front of you, taking action will always require some degree of trust.

The first trust question – do you trust yourself? – isn't looking for an absolute answer. I wonder if any of us can truly trust ourselves completely – that seems to be unrealistic. Thus, we make a slight change in this trust question. The question isn't just do you trust yourself, but rather *do you trust yourself enough?* Do you trust yourself *enough* to move forward? Do you trust yourself *enough* to take action? Do you trust yourself *enough* to take one step? Too often we think of decisions as requiring us to take a leap across some giant chasm (picture *Indiana Jones and the Last Crusade*), but this is rarely the case. More often, and no matter how big the ultimate objective is, the first step is a small step, and most decisions can and must be broken down into small steps.

I often experience people who are getting caught up in and intimidated by the seemingly big challenge or issue in front of them, but a huge challenge is rarely what's truly in front of them. Rather, there may be a big question or issue further down the road, but right now there's only a small amount of information needed, and only a small decision is required. You can certainly apply this same process to big decisions that are actually right in front of you, but most of the time your big fears will disappear or dissipate once you reframe your questions into the small decisions and steps that are required right now.

Do you trust yourself enough? I'm confident that most of the time your answer will be a resounding yes, yes, yes!

The other important trust question may be a little more difficult because it relates to the much larger realm of all the people, things and outcomes that you don't control. As already shared above, you control very little (only you), and the question of whether you trust yourself *enough* is primarily limited to your own steps. However, there's always the reality that many things are beyond your control (and perhaps even your influence), and then the trust question becomes the following: Do you trust that everything, including you, will be okay? Even if you don't get or achieve the desired result or outcome, do you believe that things and you will be okay? To be sure, I'm not using the word "okay" to suggest some form of settling or just getting by, but it is something akin to surviving.

If you've lived life much at all, you've had setbacks and failures in your life. As I often share, I've had some significant personal and professional setbacks in my life (e.g. broken marriage, damaged family relationships including with my sons, failed business, bankruptcy etc.). I took some big falls and not only got bruised but broke some bones and suffered and caused lots of heart damage. But I survived. I was okay. I stood back up, climbed back up and rose up. This isn't about trusting that everything will work out, because not everything does work out (certainly not the way we want or hope, at least). It's simply about trusting that no matter what the outcomes, you and everything will be okay. In fact, you, me and everything is *already okay*.

This is definitely not about doing nothing or simply hoping that things work out – it's about getting clear on who you are and what you want, being honest about your fears, being decisive and taking clear action and trusting that no matter what the outcomes, you and every-thing will be okay. If you're feeling the need to ask me, "How do you know?" then you're missing the point. Trust isn't about knowing – it's about, well, trusting. I don't trust because it's always true – *I trust, and it's always been true.*

I didn't see this earlier in my life, and I was quick to point out how things hadn't worked out the way I'd hoped, but I missed the truth that things had somehow worked out. Yes, it was sometimes painful, chal-lenging and scary. Yes, it was sometimes sad and lonely. And yes, it and I were always somehow okay and able to carry on. Until your, my and our last breath, we can always keep moving – choosing not to be lost or stuck. Choosing to move through our fears. Choosing to take action. Choosing to trust.

My trust continues to grow, not because the outcomes are more cer-tain, but because things and I are always okay. I've also come to accept (a form of surrender) that I don't control much, and I certainly don't con-trol outcomes. I continue to care, assess, face my fears, commit and take action, controlling the narrow universe of me that I control, including what I choose to learn from setbacks and failures. If you're looking for proof that trust works, you won't find it. Trust doesn't work because it's provable, trust works because it works.

There's the old saying that "seeing is believing," but what's more true is that "believing is seeing." If you want more proof of the truth of trust, then look back over your life. No matter what you've gone through to date, you're still here, and you're okay. You and your life may not be what you had wanted or hoped for, but we're not assured of either what we want or what we hope for. It's naïve to believe that life is designed to deliver you whatever you want, but it's wise to believe that life will deliver what you need, even if it doesn't fit what you think it should be.

The source of my deep level of trust is two-fold. First, I have a strong belief in God which provides comfort no matter what the circumstances or outcomes. Second, my trust is based upon a lifetime of proof in the form of the outcomes in my life, as well as a reframing of what it means to be okay. My younger brother Gregg was tragically killed when he was nineteen years old, which not only changed the course of my family but inflicted some deep wounds inside of me that I've only begun healing in the past nine years. Despite all of this and the sadness that every member of my family has carried since that day in 1980, we're all okay. Yes, it had a profound impact on my parents and, I believe, their marriage and relationship. Yes, my Mom lived the rest of her life carrying around deep grief that I don't believe she ever dealt with, and which I believe ultimately led to her death. Despite all of these things that most of us would label as negative outcomes (I don't like labels), life went on for all of us and everyone is okay, even though my parents' marriage ended and even though my Mom died.

As for me, my choices in life have created all sorts of outcomes that I didn't desire and which I would love to have changed, but despite it all I'm okay, I'm healing and many of those outcomes are healing. I made choices in my marriage that hurt my wife and my sons, and which led to the marriage ending, yet my relationship with my sons has been healing since I took responsibility and started to show up differently with them (in the ways I'm sharing in this book). My relationship with my wife is not healing, but I have done everything that I can to heal that relationship, and I've let go of the need to have it healed. I can't control her choices and emotions, but I can choose not to be defined by her choices.

I've had a failed business, filed bankruptcy and had to dig out from a financial catastrophe that caused all sort of pain, but I'm still here and continuing to build a thriving business. It's not perfect and I'm not perfect, but everything is still okay despite the depths of what came before. I've lost friends and family to death (some young and some old). I've lost clients and had scary times in my business. I've loved and lost and felt the deep pain of those lost relationships. I've been in the fire and at times felt like my life was on fire, and yet here I am – alive and living life full-on no matter what the outcomes. I sometimes get what I want, but often I don't, and I'm still okay and everything is okay.

Here's what you need to know about being okay. First, okay is not the same as settling. Settling is a matter of choice – choosing to settle for okay or mediocre. Second, what I'm referring to is knowing that even if things don't turn out the way you want or hope, you and things will still be okay. I'm often challenged by people who say that it's easy for me to be peaceful and to have little or no stress *because everything is working out for me*. In other words, they believe (and want to believe) that the outcomes determine my state of mind and way of being, but the opposite is true. My state of mind and way of being is independent of the outcomes, and I face significant challenges, setbacks and losses every day. Despite the outcomes, my life is filled with joy and peace. And yes, I feel sadness, anger, fear and sometimes shame, but only when I'm not present and only when I fail to trust that everything will be okay – in fact, everything is already okay.

I sometimes get what I want, but often I don't, and I'm still okay and everything is okay.

We all listen to and sing along with the Rolling Stones lyrics from "You Can't Always Get What You Want":

> No, you can't always get what you want
> You can't always get what you want
> You can't always get what you want
> But if you try sometime you find
> You get what you need

We know these lyrics well, but what if they're real and true? What if you'll always get what you need, even if it's very different from what you envisioned? Whatever you get, you get to decide if it's okay and if you're okay with it – not by settling or giving up, but by trusting the outcomes, by trusting that there's a plan beyond you, and then taking whatever next action you desire to move from one outcome to the next possibility. One step and one choice at a time.

This chapter has been about lostness, stuckness and choices, especially the acknowledgement that we always have choices and that being lost or stuck is a choice – your choice. It's also about the reality that life is meant to be an adventure, and when you're on an adventure, exploring is a major part of the journey. When others might be lost, you can instead choose to see it as part of the adventure and keep exploring. When others feel stuck and want to stop, you can choose to see it as a twist in the trail and hack your way through it. When the world seems to block your path, you can choose a different trail and find your way. When you're faced with the road well-traveled, you can trust that someone else paved that way as their own way and decide instead to take the road less traveled – your road.

Sometimes on your journey, when you're feeling stuck or in a rut, getting out of it often requires that you make a hard turn of the wheel. It's difficult to get out of a rut when you turn gently – you often need to jerk the wheel in a different direction. That's a reality of change because there are so many obstacles to changes – things and people that will try to hold you on the current course and to keep you with them, where it's familiar, comfortable and safe.

No matter your age, life situation or past experience, today is a new day filled with choices in every moment. 86,400 seconds are given to you today, for you to use or misuse, to grasp or to let slip away. No one is promised a smooth or easy ride, but we're all promised an adventure. At the end of the movie *Hook*, Wendy says to Peter Pan, "So, your adventures are over," to which Peter profoundly replies: "Oh no. To live, to live would be an awfully big adventure." I invite each one of you to live, to embrace life's big adventure, to bravely step into the unknown of life, to trust and to *Just Explore*.

Chapter 10

Just Say No

My journey to the Camino happened because I said "Yes," over and over. I said yes to the intuition I had when I saw the movie *The Way* and heard the Camino's call. I said yes when I had the opportunity to work with Mark Leblanc as a coach, knowing that he could also mentor me for my Camino journey. I said yes when I took the opportunity to ask Mark for his support around my Camino journey. I said yes when Mark shared with me that I could do the Camino in a different way – not all of it at once and earlier than I'd expected. I said yes to the Camino in May of 2017, despite the fact that it meant leaving for two weeks after an incredibly full schedule in May and knowing that there'd be challenges in being away and going offline for two weeks. And I said yes to the many adventures and experiences on the Camino by intentionally not making lodging arrangements in advance. Plenty of yes's created what became a profound journey on the Camino, which I'm sure makes you wonder why this chapter is about the "No." Simple: because every Camino "yes" was connected to an important "no," and those no's were just as (if not more) critical to my Camino experience – and a reminder for all of us of the power of the no.

Despite the powerful connection I felt to the movie *The Way* that supported the yes (I'll do it), there was a big no – saying no to comfort and old stories about doing something as big as the Camino. This includes an inside story I carry that says that such a journey is for other people (not me) and that I have to wait until everything is perfect first. When I was bidding on the coaching package with Mark, I said "no" when the bidding exceeded what I was willing to pay ($5,000), which led to me securing Mark's coaching and mentoring support at my chosen amount. I said no to the concerns I had about having a very full month of May 2017 and then taking two weeks right after that to leave my business behind to pursue an experience. Before I'd even booked my trip, I said no to other business opportunities that were offered to me for the time that I was hoping to do the Camino. Opportunities to achieve business success and revenue were presented, but I said no. In addition, I had a speaking engagement scheduled in early June, which I'd already committed to, but I took the risk of reaching out to the client to tell them I couldn't do the engagement (literally taking money off the table) due to my Camino trip. Yes was a big factor in my Camino journey, and yes, many thoughtful no's allowed it to become a reality.

There was also a big no that I chose during my Camino walk, a no that allowed the Camino to be all that it was meant to be and, I believe, even more than it ever would have been without this critical no. It was clear to me that my Camino journey was meant to be one of solitude – something that I needed to make on my own. In fact, six weeks before I left, I was talking to one of my mentors, and he asked me if it would be possible to create some alone space to be on my own. In response, I said "Do you mean like going to Spain to walk the Camino de Santiago for two weeks alone?" Yes, it was clearly designed to be a solo journey, but I quickly learned that the Camino can easily become a community experience.

As I shared earlier in this book, I met several people on my first official night on the Camino (after surviving the thunder and hailstorm and finding a place to stay). I learned from David that an informal group of fellow pilgrims had formed along their way, and they typically arranged to meet for dinner each night. I have to admit that I was drawn to this idea of having other people to connect with, whether while walking during the day or at the end of the day to share experiences and laughs. I experienced this sense of community firsthand the next day.

I'd walked for some time with a fascinating man (Alex) from Holland. Once we separated, I soon arrived at a café strategically located at the top of a long hill – when you're tired, thirsty and hungry, it's the perfect time to stop to rest, cool off, hydrate and nurture yourself (including having a cup of coffee or a beer). David and his father were at this stopover with a large group of their pilgrim friends – all sharing the day's experience together and already talking about their plans that evening. It felt good to sit with them a bit, to feel less alone and to feel like I was part of a group, and when I left them to continue my walk for the day I could feel the desire to be part of such a group.

That day, I walked a little further than most people would walk in a day, and even though I ran into David and his group later and walked with them for a short time, I walked farther than they had planned to go. The next morning, I realized that I'd likely not see David and his group again because I had outwalked them. Without consciously intending it, I'd outwalked the people that I met, thereby creating a solitude experience on the Camino. The key no in this unconscious decision was saying no to connection, no to community and no to my comfort zone. Yes, I'd meet many amazing people on my Camino journey, typically walking with them for a time on a particular day, but when we parted ways, I'd never see them again (with the exception of Roger, Tom and Adele).

The most magical gift of this no was that it was my way of saying yes to me, which is true of many of your no's as well. I learned this powerful lesson many years ago: Every yes is a no (to something or someone), and every no is a yes (often to myself). This is the amazing gift of a no, yet most of us struggle with saying no for a variety of reasons, including our need to be liked or accepted, our desire to be seen as valuable, our fear of rejection and our own insecurities. This chapter is about finding a path to more no's in your life (or at least more conscious yes's) and the recognition that healthy boundaries not only help you to serve your higher purpose, but also send an impactful message to yourself – that you're worthy.

Every yes is a no (to something or someone), and every no is a yes (often to myself).

Yes Is Easy, Boundaries Are Hard

When I speak to audiences, I often ask them how many of them are great at saying "yes" to others, and an overwhelming number of hands go up. I then ask how many of them are great at saying "yes" to themselves, and I'm lucky to see a handful of hands. Similarly, when I ask a group how many people are good at saying "no," I typically see a small number of hands in the air. What's the problem, and why is the no so difficult? We often say and think that saying "yes" is just a form of being helpful, and "isn't it a good thing to be helpful?" Nice try folks – while being giving and helpful can be a good trait, always saying yes isn't about being help-ful – it's often about being unable or unwilling to say no. Another way to look at it is to remember that when you always give by saying "yes," the thing you're giving away the most is yourself.

The last time I checked, each of us always has a limited amount of time, focus and energy, and what we do with it all has a profound impact on what we create (or not), the relationships we build (or not), the impact we have (or not) and our level of personal fulfillment (or not). Thus, getting back to the truth stated above, *every yes is a no to something or someone.* As much as we want to believe that we're skilled at multi-tasking, there's a reality of the limits of time and energy. If you say yes to a phone call at 2:00 PM today, reality dictates that you can't do something else or have another call at that same time. If you say yes to going to a movie with your partner tomorrow night, you won't be spending time tomorrow night with other friends and family. Choices and impact are a reality of our yes's and our no's, but a reality that we rarely pay attention to.

Before I go on, let me be clear and transparent – I'M A YES MAN! I've worked and continue to work on this in my life, and it's been difficult work. I've gotten so much better, and I've been guided by a few simple concepts that I'll share in the next section. One of the biggest shifts for me is to look at "no" in the context of boundaries and understanding that saying no is an act of setting boundaries. The problem for me and likely many of you is that the "yes" is easy and the "no" is hard, in large part because we don't believe that we're worthy of boundaries (i.e. looking out for ourselves, taking care of ourselves, choosing ourselves and even having choices). Too often, there's a voice in our head that says that we have to say yes, because that's what good and helpful people do.

Plus, I want to be liked and certainly don't want to be rejected, and the yes feels like the safest way to ensure being liked and not rejected. What a false story all of this is! Yes, it's true that some people may not like you and may even reject you if you say no to them, but it's also true that who you are and what you think of yourself is independent of the judgments of others. Easier said than acted on, but nonetheless true.

About a year ago I had a small but significant experience and moment of awareness that gave me a big leap forward on my journey to boundaries and saying no. I was part of a men's retreat, and I was assigned a small task to put together some information, and I'd committed to deliver it to one of the retreat leaders that morning. This leader (John) wasn't immediately available, so I asked one of the other leaders (Phil) to give the information to John. Without missing a beat, without any defensiveness or tone, and with great clarity, Phil looked me in the eye and said, "No." No preface and no explanation – just no. No justification or rationalizations – just no. I remember that my immediate response was to think, "why not – it's not a big deal," but then it hit me – that's how you say no. It was simple, clear and direct, and I loved it. While it might be easy to ask *why* Phil wasn't willing to help me out, all I know is that Phil was telling me very clearly that he wasn't willing to take on my responsibility. I was trying (without knowing it) to make delivery of the information Phil's responsibility, and he said no. It's that simple!

The biggest lesson that I've learned about boundaries is this – worthy people set healthy boundaries. Worthy people say no. Confident people say no. And yes, the opposite is largely true as well – people with worthiness doubts fail to set healthy boundaries and default to yes. Insecure people and people-pleasers default to yes. The question and awareness isn't about whether yes or no is the *right answer* – there's no right or wrong answer. The key point is to be aware of the drivers behind your yes.

Are you saying yes because you want to, or because you feel like you have to? Are you saying yes because you want to do what you're being asked to do, or because you want to be liked? Are you saying yes because you want to, or because you don't want to let the other person down? Are you saying yes because you truly want to help, or because you're afraid of being judged or rejected? Are you saying yes because you want to, or because yes is easier and more comfortable (while no is scary and uncomfortable)?

Remember, healthy boundaries (and no's) are the best way to tell yourself that you're worthy.

What's your story about yes and no and boundaries? Are you worthy of setting healthy boundaries and saying no? Are you worthy enough to say yes to yourself? Are you worthy enough to choose where you invest your time, focus and energy? Even more important, are your yes's moving you in the direction you desire to go, or are your yes's *keeping you from those desires*? Even simpler and more critically – in what ways would your path to your desires and objectives be impacted (and smoothed) by a few more no's? Remember, healthy boundaries (and no's) are the best way to tell yourself that you're worthy.

Tools for No

Given all the difficulties with no, I've found it helpful to use a few "no tools" to help you in setting boundaries and uttering that ugly, two-letter word "no." These tools will not eliminate the various challenges to the no, but they'll help you navigate a world where you're being constantly called upon for a resounding yes. There are four essential tools to support you on your journey from yes to no.

1. Pause
2. Keep it clear and simple (and without three specific words)
3. I choose to …
4. Not now

Each one of these tools will help you enhance your no muscle and, collectively, they'll work together to support you in your journey to saying no.

The pause tool is just what it sounds like – it's simply training yourself to pause before responding to someone who's asking you to do something, get involved or take responsibility for something. Actually, there's two parts to the pause tool, and the first one is easy – take a breath. What are you talking about, Jeff? Take a breath is your advice? Yes, that's exactly what I'm saying because when we're asked to do something or "help out" (those dreaded words), for most of us our immediate reaction is to say yes, even if our immediate thought and want is to say no. Think about it – when someone asks us to do something, a warning bell usually goes off in our heads: "Danger Will Robinson!" Someone is asking you to give up some of your time and freedom, and your defenses go up. Yet, most of the time the no in our thoughts comes out of our mouth as yes. Why? Because our unconscious reaction (which is where all of your doubts, worthiness questions, insecurities, fears of rejection and need for acceptance live) slips out before we have the time to be thoughtful and discerning. If you're like me, you've had many out of body experiences where you want to say no, yet you hear yourself saying yes (even as your conscious mind is screaming "Nnnnnnoooooooo").

By taking a breath (the first step) you create space for the pause – initially a brief pause, which then paves the way for a conscious and negotiated pause. The breath is what will keep that yes from leaping out of your mouth and allow you space to think about what you really want. The breath is what will slow down your automatic (and unconscious) response and allow you space for the thoughtful (and conscious) response. The breath is the bridge to answering the question (yes or no) on purpose, rather than by default.

Now let's look at the pause, which can be either a momentary pause or a longer-term pause. However, the initial pause is the key to the longer pause. While the pause can vary depending on the nature of the question and the significance of what's being asked, the key is to find the pause so that you can slow down and minimize the reactive answer (which is usually the yes). One thing to note up front is that the pause must be accompanied with either a quick response (with the short pause) or a clear commitment to a future response (with the longer pause). I'll talk more about this commitment element below. Another essential element is to remember that the pause is often followed by clarifying questions to help you better understand what exactly is being requested and, critically, assess the personal impact of a yes (e.g. impact on time, focus, energy, or other priorities).

Here's an example of a momentary pause:

- **Question:** Can you help out with the team's fundraising campaign?
- **Immediate (unconscious) Response:** Absolutely. Happy to help! [You're now in without even knowing what you've committed to. You can try to clarify or minimize your yes after the fact, but you've already said yes.]

- **Question:** Can you help out with the team's fundraising campaign?
- **Breath and Pause ...**
- **Clarifying Questions:** I do think the fundraising campaign is important. Where do you think I can be helpful, and in what specific ways would you like me to be involved?

It seems too simple and easy, but the truth is that most of our yes's jump out of us before we've really thought through what's being asked, what's expected and, most important, what's the impact in your life and world.

The longer pause usually follows the short pause (and the questions that you ask along with it) and is designed to give you time to be thoughtful and intentional. As noted above, it requires a clear commitment so that the asker knows that the pause is temporary (and not an escape hatch).

- **Question:** Can you help out with the team's fundraising campaign?
- **Breath and Pause ...**
- **Clarifying Questions:** I do think the fundraising campaign is important. In what ways do you think I can be helpful and what specific ways would you like me to be involved?

- Answer to Clarifying Questions
- **Thoughtful Response:** When I get involved in things, I'm all in, and I've learned that people often say yes without being ready to fully commit. I appreciate the invitation to be a part of this campaign, and I want [not need] a little bit of time before I can commit the way I'm sure you want me to.
- **Clear Commitment:** I commit to getting back to you with either additional questions or an answer within the next forty-eight hours. If you don't hear back from me by then, please reach out to me again.

This approach allows you to take time to be thoughtful, and it also communicates that you're taking the question and the request seriously. It also makes it clear that you're not trying to blow the person off because they'll get a clear answer in the short term. While not everyone will like this (they want a clear yes and they want it now), it's very difficult for most people not to respect your response. I'll talk more below about one of the reasons that people may seem not to respect your no, which will give you an additional tool on your journey to no. This leads us to the second tool: keep it clear and simple.

The keep it clear and simple tool is, well, clear and simple. It relates to the way that you communicate your no's and, coupled with the "I'm choosing" tool below, is an impactful shift that will help you embrace and step into the no zone.

You know you *want to say no*, but what comes out of your mouth is vague, ambiguous and slippery.

I've heard from hundreds if not thousands of people that they're frustrated by people (the askers) who seem not to respect their no, and what I've discovered is that they're wrong. Nearly everyone respects a clear no – the problem is that we're not giving clear no's. I know, I know – you *think you're being clear*, but most of the clarity is only on your end. You know you *want to say no*, but what comes out of your mouth is vague, ambiguous and slippery. Why? Because you want to avoid the risk of being clear with your no, and you hope the asker will figure it out and accept your wishy-washy answer.

Think about my example above with John and Phil – Phil's answer to my request was one word: No! No preambles, explanations, excuses or rationalizations. Honestly, it was so clear and clean that I was speechless. I had nothing to respond with or to because Phil hadn't given me anything – no hope or glimpse of a way around his no. Think about this truth when it comes to a sales situation. When you try to explain your no to a salesperson, they seem to keep digging around and working on a yes. However, when you say no (nothing more), they're far less likely to try to push you. Even with persistent sales people, when I say no and they push on, I follow it up with something clear like, "I was very clear – no." I don't have to keep coming up with other things to say; I only need to keep repeating the simple and clear word, "NO."

Most often, instead of *just saying no* (thank you, Nancy Reagan) we explain why we want to say no, but we never actually use the word no (again, hoping that the asker will infer the no for us so we don't have to say it). Here's a typical example:

- **Question:** Can you help out with the team's fundraising campaign?
- **Indirect Answer:** I'd love to help, but I've a lot going on (work, family, church, education, etc.). I do think this campaign is important, but now isn't the best time for me.

Sound familiar? Have you said similar things to askers in the past? Do you see the problem? There's a great deal being communicated in the response, but one word is missing – no! These types of responses are designed with the hope to have the asker leave you alone and answer *for you* – to effectively get them to take the ask off the table. As you probably already know, this is usually not the outcome that occurs. Instead, the asker keeps pushing for a yes, you feel that your no isn't being respected (even though you didn't say no), and the outcome is often either a begrudging yes or a defensive no. You want to blame the asker, but this is on you, my friends. You alone have the power of the no, and if you choose not to use it, then the discomfort and outcome is on you.

Part of being simple and clear includes avoiding three key words and phrases – words and phrases that sound good, but which are not only unclear but actually invite the asker to follow up and even push. These words and phrases will also help to explain the reason behind what you perceive is a lack of respect for your no (in addition to the fact that you're often not saying no).

Here are the three phrases and words to avoid when responding to any asker:

- I can't because _____
- I'm busy
- But

The first two phrases to avoid are related, especially when you want to respond, "I can't because I'm busy." This is actually the double whammy because it has two must-avoid words (can't and busy). The third phrase is just one word – but – which by itself isn't the problem. The problem is that the but almost always follows an affirmative statement and, as I learned many years ago, everything in front of the but *is a lie*.

Let's start with the first phrase: I can't. We all use it and at times even love it, but we all also know that it's a lie. Whether we talk about it or not, we all know that "can't" is the throwaway word that we often use when we really *don't want to* do something. Can't has become our supposed get out of jail free card, seemingly (we think) excusing us from anything we want to avoid. Let me clear right now – people (including askers) WILL NOT respect the can't, and it's naïve of you to expect them to.

How many times have you done, achieved or accomplished things that you thought you couldn't? The same is true for all the askers out there, including you. By the way, when you want to start to sling arrows at all the askers, remember that there are times when you're the asker. Are you learning from your experience as the asker, or are you inflicting on others what you've experienced as the askee?

No matter how much you want to believe that can't is clear, simple and true, it's time to pay the honesty piper. The truth is nearly always that saying you can't is the cover up for the fact that you're choosing not to – unless the ask conflicts specifically with some other commitment. And even then, you could still choose to say yes to this ask and say no to the prior commitment. In fact, we've all done just that many times in our lives (often based upon priorities or simply what we want to do more). This is why very few people respect the can't, and if you choose to hide behind the can't, then expect to continue to be hounded by all the askers (and appropriately so). Saying you can't is neither clear, simple nor true, and it's time to admit it.

The same truth applies to the busy excuse. Why? Because everyone is busy. The entire US population is busy at least. I'm not able to speak authoritatively about other cultures, but the American culture has embraced busy as the goal to be achieved, the top of the mountain. As such, we're all busy, and therefore responding to an ask with "I'm busy" or, even worse, "I can't because I'm busy" is almost insulting. Why would anyone respect your busyness when you wouldn't respect their busyness? The reason the busy response is insulting is because the asker is already busy. Even if you think they're not, trust **me**: they think they are, and yet they're already involved and helping. Here's the simple truth – if the asker is busy and still helping, then why can't you help *even if you're busy*? Not only will your busy response not be respected, but it's likely to result in the asker being even more persistent.

Not only will your busy response not be respected, but it's likely to result in the asker being even more persistent.

Admittedly, dumping the busy excuse will be a challenge for one simple reason – you actually believe it. You think that you're the only one that's busy and you think that being busy is all you need to say to an asker, but busy isn't an answer. Busy is an excuse and often an insulting excuse, so dump the busy.

That brings us to the word "but," which reveals everything in front of it as a lie. As noted above, but isn't the problem – the problem is what the but is paired with. Let's look at some examples, which quickly make the point:

- **Question:** Can you help out with the team's fundraising campaign?
- **But Answer:** I'd love to help, **but** I [Insert dozens of possible "reasons" (excuses) as to why you can't help (Oops, here comes the ugly "can't" again)].

While it might be true for you that you really want to help, we've been culturized to use but as an out card to avoid doing something that we don't want to do. Most of us have also had the regular occurrence of using the but (and having the but used on us) to negate whatever was said in front of it:

- I don't mean to complain, but …
- I'm a team player, but …
- I want to be with you, but …
- I take my commitments seriously, but …
- Don't take this personally, but …

I'm sure that you're seeing the point. The but has become another escape and excuse valve in so many situations that it no longer has much credibility. Thus, when you use the but word when responding to anything you've been asked, first, you shouldn't expect it to be respected and, second, you should expect that it will be seen and heard for what it most likely is – an excuse. As you'll see below in the "I choose to" section, there's an alternative to the but that's more likely to be respected (nearly always, in fact) and which is actually most true about your response.

There you have it – three words and phrases to avoid when it comes to asks and boundaries: I can't, I'm busy and but. While they feel true and clear, they're just the opposite, they will not be respected and they're keeping you from being direct, clear and honest – and from achieving what you want from your interactions.

In contrast to the foregoing phrases to avoid, the "I choose to" communication tool is simple, direct, honest and empowering. It's empowering because it's based upon a universal truth – the truth that we always have choices. They may be difficult and even seemingly impossible choices, but we always have choices, and owning your choices is something that people can and will respect (especially askers).

In simplest terms, the "I choose to" is the replacement for the can't. While can't is almost always not really true and more a matter of choices and priorities, the "I choose to" is clear, direct and honest. Let's look at some typical examples to make this point:

> **Can't:** I can't get involved with the team's campaign because I have a lot going on at work right now.
> **I Choose:** *I'm choosing not to get involved with the team's campaign because of my current work commitments.*

> **Can't:** I can't get involved with the team's campaign because I have a lot going on at home.
> **I Choose:** *I'm choosing not to get involved with the team's campaign because I'm making a choice to spend more time with my family.*

> **Can't:** I can't get involved with the team's campaign because I have a conflict this month.
> **I Choose:** *I'm choosing not to get involved with the team's campaign because I've already committed to work on a project at home this month and I'm choosing to honor that commitment.*

Imagine if you were the asker and someone was honest with their choices and priorities in this way and made it clear that they were choosing something else. You may not like the answer (because you wanted a yes), but it's extremely difficult not to respect it and even more difficult to keep pushing for a yes in the face of an honest communication of choice. This is even more true when you state your response in terms of honoring other and prior commitments. People and askers will typically respect honesty, choices and commitments, and the clear no. If you're wondering, there's a clear no in each of the above examples: "I'm choosing **not to**."

Trust me, when you choose to be simple, clear and direct, when you avoid certain words and phrases (can't, busy and but), and you own your choices and commitments, you'll find not only that your no's are respected, but that you'll get fewer and fewer pushes. Admittedly, implementing the foregoing "no tools" can still be challenging, and (no but here!) these tools will help you set more boundaries and deliver more no's *despite some of the old voices that caused you to say yes when you really wanted to say no.*

These tools will help you set more boundaries and deliver more no's *despite some of the old voices that caused you to say yes when you really wanted to say no.*

Okay then, I know that you're all asking one question – and of course you start with a but – *but what about work?* You're right that all of my examples above related to a non-work question; however, the same tools apply at work. The only question is whether you're willing to take the initial risks. The ultimate risk is the no because we believe that if we're asked to do something at work, we have to say yes. This is a lie.

Good (not even great) leaders and managers are more concerned about getting things done than about having people say they'll do something (and then not getting it done). If you say "yes" at work but don't follow through, it's a failure for everyone – you, your manager, the team and the organization – and trust is broken and depleted. Leaders and managers would rather you say "no" or "not now" to open the door to a conversation about realistic expectations and commitments. If your manager is not open to hearing a genuine no or not know, then there's an issue with their leadership. Any manager who wants you to say "yes" to make them feel better (even if it's not realistic) is failing in their leadership.

Yes, there are bad managers and leaders out there, and one of the best ways to find out which you're working with is to practice all of the no tools above. You can assume the worst of others, but the only way to know for sure is to take the risk (even in small doses) to give people a chance to be and lead differently. If you're uncertain, then try these tools out in small doses at work. Another way to dip your toe in the water is to breathe, pause and ask this priority clarification **question:** *Can we spend a few minutes talking about where this request fits in your priorities and my priorities?* You'll likely be surprised at the ways that such a question is respected and responded to.

Now we come to one of the truly amazing no tools – not now. Whether explicitly asked or implied, we tend to experience requests as if the only answers are yes or no, which is stressful and limiting. We forget that there's a third and fourth option. The third option is to clarify what's being asked, so that your answer may be different. The fourth option is the not now, as evidenced below:

- **Question:** Can you help out with the team's fundraising campaign?
- **Not Now Answer:** I want to help, and the campaign is important. I have several other priorities over the next two weeks, and I'm willing to get involved later this month.

- **Question:** Can you help out with the team's fundraising campaign?
- **Not Now Answer:** I want to help, and the campaign is important. I have several other priorities over the next few months, and I'm happy to get involved with next year's campaign.

To be clear, your not now responses must be honest and represent a true commitment. These aren't throwaways (call me next year) – they're clear, direct and honest commitments to help, just not right now.

I'm finding that the not now response is one of my greatest no tools. When someone asks for a phone call or meeting, and there are myriad reasons that doing it right now (e.g. today, this week or even this month) isn't in my best interests, I'll often say, "I'd love to get together. Let's do it next month." I often instinctively want to say yes, but a yes right now isn't the best choice for many reasons. Rather than saying yes when I don't actually want to, making excuses or saying no when I want to say yes,

I rely on the not now. I've found that people / askers readily respect the not now. If they feel like the matter is pressing, they'll typically share it with me and we'll have a direct and honest conversation about priorities. Rarely does someone push me or fail to respect my not now, and the same will be true for you.

There you have it – the four essential no tools: 1. Pause; 2. Keep it clear and simple (and avoid the never words); 3. Own your choices; and 4. Remember the not now. While the no may always be challenging for each of you, these tools will help you more successfully navigate the minefield of askers and requests in every nook and cranny of your life.

Your T Factor

In the past couple of years, I've found an aspect of our life and leadership that's not getting enough attention, and it's an area that's directly related to the no zone and boundaries. We often think of no's and boundaries as only coming into play when a direct ask is being made, but this is only one aspect of boundaries. Another aspect has to do with the people, situations and behavior that we allow, refuse to say no to and, therefore, tolerate. This brings us to the T factor – the tolerance factor – which has led me to this truth:

> "Your leadership, your relationships, your life and your impact are not defined by what you preach, *but by what and who you tolerate.*"

I've gotten a great deal of pushback and resistance to this position over the past two years – not denying its truth but offering up all the "reasons" for the tolerance. That's the challenging thing about this truth – reasons (aka excuses) don't change the fact of the tolerance and its impact. In fact, I'd say that the things, people, situations and behaviors that you tolerate in your life and leadership have the most profound impact and are the biggest obstacle to you having what you want and achieving your objectives.

How does the tolerance factor relate to the boundaries and the no zone? It's simple: whatever you're tolerating is an outcome of you *failing or refusing to set boundaries and to say no.* No to certain people. No to certain situations. No to certain behaviors. I'm sure you've all heard before about having a zero-tolerance policy for something (e.g. zero tolerance on drugs at work), but do you have a zero-tolerance zone with friends, family, communication or behaviors? If not, now is the time to start thinking about and implementing zero (or at least limited) tolerance zones in various parts of your life.

Make a list right now – what and who are you tolerating right now? Are you clear that you're tolerating it or them? Do you fully understand why you're tolerating it or them? What's the cost of you tolerating it or them? I'll walk you through a tolerance assessment and action process below, but for now I want you to be honest about the tolerance that you're exhibiting in your life – all because of your failure or refusal to set healthy boundaries and to say no.

Do you have family or friends who seem to insist on bringing negative or even toxic conversations, drama and energy into your life and interactions? What would a healthy boundary and saying no look like here?

Do you have people or situations at work that are keeping you either from achieving your goals or from enjoying your work? What would a healthy boundary and saying no look like in your work world?

Do you have partners or relationships that are causing stress, impacting your joy or diminishing your other relationships? What would a healthy boundary and saying no look like in your life?

What you're tolerating is likely having more of an impact on you, your life and your trajectory than anything else,

Tolerance is a reality, and boundaries and no's are the solution. Are you ready to take a look at what you're tolerating, believe enough in yourself to set some healthy boundaries, and start saying no, even without a question being asked? As I noted above, what you're tolerating is likely having more of an impact on you, your life and your trajectory than anything else, and it's up to you to choose to take action to reduce or eliminate the tolerance with intentional boundaries and no's.

A Tolerance Process

If you want to change your tolerance factor and dynamics, you'll need a process. What follows is a series of steps to help you assess, discern and decide what to do (or not do) with your tolerance factor. Even if you choose to keep your tolerance factor where it is, the process of assessing the tolerance and its impact, and making a conscious decision on what to change (or not), will help you to reduce your stress, improve your outcomes and experience a compelling sense of empowerment in every part of your life.

I admit that there might be long-held beliefs or reasons for your tolerance, and certainly there are always risks or fears that drive our tolerance. As a result, I've gotten many questions about what to do about tolerance. I'm not naïve, and I'm not suggesting that everyone (including you) must immediately stop tolerating everything they currently tolerate (although that might be the answer).

Rather than leave you dangling with your tolerance, I've developed the following six-step assessment process for you to use for your tolerance (your "T" factor).

1. **Assess the Tolerance** – This involves getting clear, specific and honest with yourself about exactly what you're tolerating. This isn't the time to focus on the reasons or excuses for the tolerance – just be honest about exactly what you're tolerating in people, situations or behaviors. It's critical that you be very specific with this step. For example, you're not tolerating a "bad employee." You must be clear about what specific behaviors by this employee that you're tolerating.

2. **Assess the Impact** – While this may seem like an easy process, most of you probably have never gotten clear on all of the impacts that are flowing from your tolerance. This again is time to be really honest about the impact (both direct and indirect) that your tolerance is creating.

3. **Assess the Risks** – This relates to the reasons and excuses that you've been making to justify your tolerance. We typically

tolerate things, people and situations because of the risks and fears associated with taking action to reduce or eliminate whatever is being tolerated. The best question to ask for this part of the process is, "Why am I choosing to tolerate this person, situation or behavior?" Focus on the risks – what you're afraid might happen – of addressing or ending the tolerance. One very important point is to not accept or stop with your first answers. Your first few answers to these questions are usually the most exaggerated (and least likely to occur). They're also the answers designed to keep you in your comfort zone and to justify you not making any changes. Keep asking and answering this question about risks until you get to what's most real and true.

4. **Assess the Win** – This is something many of you never do when it comes to tolerance. It involves focusing on the specific wins (the benefits) that will occur if you choose to reduce or eliminate whatever you're currently tolerating. In other words, in what ways will things be better without the tolerance?

5. **Consciously Choose** – Now that you know the real costs of your tolerance, what the risks and fears are, and what the wins and benefits of reducing or ending the tolerance are, it's time to choose. Consciously choose whether to continue the tolerance or to take different actions to eliminate or modify the tolerance. Most of your tolerance is happening without you ever fully contemplating the foregoing areas, and once you've gotten this far in the assessment process you'll be in the best position to make a clear choice – to continue to tolerate or to eliminate (or diminish) the tolerance. At a minimum, you'll now be making a clear and conscious decision instead of a default reaction to people, situations or behaviors.

6. **Let It Go** – This is a big one. Once you make a clear and conscious choice regarding your tolerance, even if you decide to continue with the tolerance, let the decision go and live with it and its impacts. Once you've consciously decided to continue

with tolerance, there's nothing more to fret about or con- template – you've decided to tolerate and to experience the impacts. While your tolerance has impacts, it makes no sense to continue to worry about your tolerance if you're consciously choosing to tolerate with full awareness of the impacts, risks and potential wins. This also means no more talking about it. This is a waste of time and energy after you've decided to continue the tolerance. Decide and then let it go!

Claim your life and your leadership by owning your tolerance and decide!

That's it – a systematic approach and process to assessing your tolerance, the drivers of it, the opportunities beyond it, and the opportunity to make a clear choice. That's what leaders do in their businesses, with their teams and in their lives.

You may continue to tolerate, but take this big step forward by fully and honestly assessing your tolerance. Claim your life and your leader- ship by owning your tolerance and decide!

The "No" Feels Good

Go on… admit it. It feels good – no, it feels GREAT – to say no! Think about the last time you said no to someone or something else and thereby said YES to you and to your priorities. Damn, that felt good, didn't it? While the process of getting to no can be difficult, especially in the beginning, the no zone tools above will support you on your no journey. Even if it's challenging and even risky (there are no guarantees in life, my friends), the good feeling that comes with a boundary and a no comes for obvious reasons. Simply put, when you set healthy boundaries and say no to others and to tolerances, you're saying yes to someone very special – YOU! Even more important, these no's to others and yes's to you are a loud and proud statement of the following – You're Worthy!

You're good enough on your own, and you don't need to be liked and accepted by others. You're good enough even if you say no. You're more than your yes's. You're good enough without doing it all. At the core of the core, you're enough. That's the starting point, and those who are already enough are those who set healthy boundaries and say no.

I said yes many times to get to the Camino, but the profundity of my Camino experience was formed by the most important no – no to connection, no to comfort zones, no to community. My many no's on the Camino granted me a yes to solitude and aloneness. What a gift – a gift that I'm offering to you in this book. I wonder what my experience would have been if I'd said yes to finding my Camino tribe? I know it wouldn't have been as deep, profound and impactful as it was on my own. This book and everything that I'm sharing with you wouldn't be happening, and I wouldn't have all of this to offer you if I'd said yes to community on the Camino. The no had its lonely moments, and that was the gift – a gift that continues to bless me every day for the rest of my life.

This I know in my heart. You're enough. You're worthy. *Just say no!*

Chapter 11

Just Why

I shared with you in Chapter 3 (Just The Facts) about the painful issues I endured on the Camino with my ankles and feet. First, there were the two shin splints that I encountered (my left shin on day two and my right shin on day three). Even more significant were the painful problems that developed on the balls of both my feet starting on day three, which were with me for every step on the Camino starting that day. The typical pain level was four to six, but when I stumbled on a rock and didn't land just right ... pain off the charts that literally brought me to tears. This was the painful challenge I faced for nearly all of my Camino journey; a challenge that proved to be one of my greatest teachers from my experiences. And this painful reality of my journey has caused so many people to ask, "How did you do it?" and "Why didn't you quit?"

Most people have two guesses to answer the question of why I didn't quit. First, because I'd come so far for this big adventure that I wasn't going to quit or shorten the journey. After all, I'd come so far, planned so much and paid so much to be there. Good guess, but no. Second, because I'm persistent and I just gutted it out to finish, despite the painful challenges. An even better guess because I'm the type of person that would do that – gut it out – but this is also not the answer.

When I was sharing this story with my good friends Thom and Mary, and had shared the foregoing questions and guesses, I noticed that Thom had a big smile on his face. When I asked him what he was grinning about, he said, "I know the answer. It never crossed your mind to shorten your trip or quit. It wasn't even part of your thinking." And Thom is precisely

My Camino experience only deepened these beliefs and clarified how impactful your why will be in helping you not only to overcome, but to achieve – even to be unstoppable.

right – I never considered quitting or shortening my journey, and the reason for this is simple – *my why negated all possible what's and how's.* My why – my purpose and mission (and I truly was on a mission) – overcame all the pain, so much so that even the pain became just a part of the experience and not something to overcome or endure. It was just there, with me, as part of my Camino journey and experience.

I already had strong beliefs about the power of the why before I went to the Camino, and my Camino experience only deepened these beliefs and clarified how impactful your why will be in helping you not only to overcome, but to achieve – even to be unstoppable. Remember that unstoppable doesn't mean that you never stop or rest, but that you'll always carry on and continue as you chase down your dreams and desires. Your why is one of the key ingredients to your unstoppable you.

Camino Whys

My Camino journey was filled with so many different whys, whether they were the whys that took me to Spain or the whys that presented themselves while I was on the Camino. As I shared at the outset, my why began when I synchronistically watched the movie *The Way* in that hotel in Raleigh, NC. My why deepened as I learned more and more about the Camino experience. My why deepened again when I took the risk to engage Mark Leblanc as my coach and mentor, and I felt my why say "yes" when I learned that I could do a part of the Camino in May of 2017.

My why gained profound momentum as I stayed open and *just listened* as everything in my life lined up for me to take this Camino journey. My why – mostly an intuitive sense more than a conscious thought or decision – had been drawing me to the Camino for two years. As Mark shared with me in his home in December 2016, he saw the look in my eye and knew that I was going to make the journey because *I'd been called by the Camino.* That call was the voice of my why, even if I didn't fully understand it and wouldn't understand it until I was on the Camino and, in some ways, many months later. My undefined why was at the heart of my journey to the Camino, and it was there in northern Spain that I encountered so many other whys that unfolded inside me.

One of my other intentional pre-Camino whys was to escape – not to escape my life, but to escape the ways I've always done things. To escape my connections to people. To escape my connection to the world through technology and social media. To escape what I've always known. To escape my daily distractions of information. To escape myself and my own mind. To find a way to slow down my experience of life so that I can more deeply experience my life. All of these are different forms of the why of escape.

It was on the Camino that so many other whys unfolded and flooded around, through and within me. Yes, I knew that one key why of the journey and calling was the need to be in solitude and to take this adventure alone. I also knew that one why was to push outside my comfort zone in many ways. I'm fairly low maintenance when it comes to travel, so the sleeping arrangements were never a concern to me, and I had made the purposeful decision not to make reservations on the Camino, so I was prepared for those uncertainties. And while I'd already begun to embrace significant travel experiences on my own in 2016 when I went to Hawaii alone, this trip to Spain was my first trip to Europe in nearly twenty years. I'd convinced myself that traveling to Europe was somehow a big deal and something you had to really plan for, but I realized through my Camino adventure that one why was to understand the simplicity of travel – even to other countries and continents.

Thanks to the Camino, I now see travel to far-away places as nothing more than booking a flight and having an up-to-date passport. Certainly I was also aware in advance that my Camino experience was part of a why of living and experiencing a journey into the unknown, without the normal comforts of life – to carry my world with me on my back for those two weeks and to make my way and figure it out every day, just one step at a time. These were some of the whys that I was aware of *before* the Camino, but so many more whys showed themselves to me while I was on the Camino.

As noted in the Just Say No chapter, aloneness and solitude were part of my why for this Camino journey, but this why went much deeper. Not only was I physically alone much of the time, but I also chose to experience the Camino free of every possible distraction. Not only did I walk alone most of the time, but I chose not to listen to anything on my phone – no music, no audiobooks and no podcasts. Similarly, I didn't take any books with me and didn't do any reading for the entire two weeks. My only interaction with the written word was what I wrote in my leather-bound journal every evening, as I chronicled the experiences, thoughts and people from each day. I also chose to disconnect from my business, with the exception of no more than fifteen minutes of checking emails at the end of each day. As the only person that was part of my business at the time, I checked emails every day, but I didn't respond to any emails or return any calls until after I returned. Likewise, I didn't engage with social media while I was gone other than a maximum of fifteen minutes every day to post a comment or video specifically about my Camino journey and experience. While these may seem like small steps, they were big shifts for me and all part of my why of solitude, separation and worldly disconnection.

This why and its resulting intentional decisions created an outcome that fed into another why – time and space to be present and ponder whatever came to me. I've devoted an entire upcoming chapter to the most precious lesson that I brought back from the Camino – the power and magic of full presence – but here I'll say simply that being present during every step of my Camino allowed me to have the experience of in-the-moment thoughts. Another element of this why was the pause – the conscious choice not only to slow down your pace, but to embrace and create pauses in your daily experiences. Whether your pauses are in conversations to minimize your emotional reactions, pausing in your decision-making as described in the Just Say No chapter or literally just pausing during your day, the impact of the pause on your daily experiences, your presence and your relationships will be palpable. And all of these outcomes follow from your intentional whys that are put into practice.

Whether they were about something I was seeing or experiencing, or about something that popped into my mind, my Camino journey was like a flowing river of contemplation, ponderings and thoughts. It was an experience of connection with my thoughts and intuitions that I've never before experienced, and it offered me profound levels of clarity and discernment.

> It was as if I was walking through a process of growing wisdom without any plan or instruction, and it was real.

It was as if I was walking through a process of growing wisdom without any plan or instruction, and it was real.

Another why that surfaced through my Camino experience was the intentional and often conscious act of facing my fears and getting outside my comfort zone, whether those fears be external and experiential or internal and emotional. Nothing about the Camino was my normal. In fact, this was a typical set of questions that I was asked before I left for the Camino (and my answers):

- Do you regularly travel to Europe? *No, only once before, in 1999.*
- Have you ever been to Spain? *No.*
- Have you ever hiked a long distance with a pack? *Not since a Boy Scout hike on the Appalachian Trail when I was 15.*
- Have you ever carried all of your gear for any period of time? *Again, not since I was 15.*
- Have you ever stayed in a hostel or albergue? *No.*
- Do you speak much Spanish? *No.*
- Have you ever hiked 15 to 20 miles a day? *No.*
- Have you ever hiked more than 150 miles? *No.*
- Have you ever taken such a solitude journey? *No.*
- Have you ever spent this much time alone? *No.*

One person in particular asked me these questions before I left and, when I finished answering, she said (with a smile), "It's all new and you're okay with all of it. You're crazy!" You get the point – none of my upcoming experience was typical of anything I'd done before, and I was choosing to step into my uncomfortable, my unknown and my fears. All part of a why to have an experience outside of the normal and to see in what ways it would touch me and teach me.

There are three other whys that showed themselves during my Camino journey – none of which were really planned or expected, but all of which I clearly was meant to experience. These three were letting go, God and grief. Yes, I'd contemplated and planned to bring along a couple of stones for things that I wanted to let go of in my life, but several of my letting go moments that occurred on the Camino were unplanned and unanticipated. One, a relationship, I thought that I'd already let go of, but it was only on the Camino that I realized that there was more to let go, and I did let that last bit go.

The God why was differently unanticipated. While God is a definitive part of my life, beliefs, faith and journey, I had no idea how profoundly and often the God why would surface, but I'm not at all surprised. This kind of profound aloneness and often silence is precisely the time when I'd expect God to speak to me the most – in the stillness and in his still, small voice. In Chapter 3 (Just the Facts), I shared with you my early experience with God in the midst of the lightning and hailstorm while walking along the top of the ridge on my first day. That moment – asking for God's assurance that he "had this" and feeling the immediate relief of knowing that God had it and me in his hands – was the beginning of so many different God moments throughout the Camino.

I shouldn't be surprised that God kept showing up for and with me throughout the Camino journey, whether it was answering a prayer for comfort, a sense that I was protected throughout the journey or the many people and experiences that were a part of my every day on the Camino. I felt a palpable connection to and with God throughout my journey, and this wasn't something that I had anticipated or looked for. God just kept showing up, which is precisely how I believe that God works. So, God was a why for my Camino adventure and experience, even though I didn't realize it until later. As I read many years ago, when Joseph Jaworski was asked whether God was a part of an experience that was being discussed, he answered: "Whether invoked or not, God is present." (*Synchronicity: The Inner Path of Leadership*, 2011). And God was definitely present (whether invoked or not) and a beautiful why on the Camino.

The most unexpected why for me on the Camino was the why of grief. Grief wasn't a key element of my life before the Camino, and I had no thoughts about grief before I began my journey. Yet grief became my constant companion on the Camino, starting with waking up on the second morning to the news of my Uncle Chuck's death. It continued with a conversation with Dennis (the Anglican priest) on the third morning, who shared with me that during his Camino journey, a virtual stranger had held him while he wailed with grief from the recent death of his father. Grief presented itself again later on when I walked with Henry from Germany and he shared with me that his mother had died while he was on the Camino, yet he'd chosen not to return home, trusting that their relationship had been healed before he left and that she knew he was right where he belonged.

Grief also hit close to home on the sixth day when I got a text that the son of one of my good friends had died suddenly (only in his thirties). I couldn't imagine the depth of the pain of that grief, and I was sad that I wasn't there to support him. I was also angry at the death of such a young man. I remember feeling again the connection with grief on this journey, and I wrote in my journal: "Grief is stalking me on the Camino." Shortly after this news, I met and walked with a twenty-one-year-old named Damian (from Poland and England), and we talked about life, careers and choices. Damian

My Camino was a walk with grief, another unexpected why, and little did I know that grief would soon become my almost constant companion.

was so full of life and had already traveled extensively throughout Europe, and I realized that he was the answer to my sadness and anger about my friend's son.

My Camino was a walk with grief, another unexpected why, and little did I know that grief would soon become my almost constant companion as a close family friend (Carla) passed away six months later, my Mom passed away seven months later, two other friends passed away within weeks of my Mom's death, my Uncle Gary passed away nine months after the Camino, and my Uncle Ivan (my Mom's last sibling) fifteen months later. While I'd certainly experienced losses in my life in the past, most notably my younger brother Gregg's death in 1980, grief wasn't a regular part of my journey, but grief came into focus on the Camino and it has been a nearly constant part of my life since then. Without knowing it, intending it or planning it, grief was a why that showed up on and in my Camino experience, and I'm deeply grateful for it. I wouldn't have wished these many losses on my family and the other families involved, but I'm grateful that grief was one of my Camino companions and teachers. The grief why of the Camino helped prepare me in so many unexpected ways for the losses that have come to me over the past two years, and this why will continue to be with me for the rest of my life's journey.

Claiming and Allowing Your Whys

As you can see with my Camino whys, there are two basic types of whys. There are the whys that you intentionally claim for yourself, and there are the whys that you allow to present themselves to you and inside of you. And there are combinations of both.

When I saw the movie *The Way* and listened to the intuitive message that said that I'd walk the Camino, it wasn't something that I consciously thought about or intended, but it showed up in the form of the movie, and I allowed it. I then claimed this why and set my sights on it in the form of intentions, commitments, planning and action. Thus, the calling that I experienced through *The Way* was a why that I allowed first and then later claimed.

In contrast, the many whys that I experienced on the Camino (e.g. letting go, grief, facing fears, God, etc.) were all whys that I was open to and which I allowed. Since returning from my journey, they've become conscious and intentional whys that I've claimed for my life and for me. I've made them part of my whole life journey, while they originally showed up on my Camino journey. There's no good and bad, better or worse when it comes to claiming and allowing whys – there's just a difference in origin.

Certainly, you can decide to embrace and claim a why in your life and then set your intentions, commitments, plans and actions around it. If you experience some new why through any life experiences and you're open to allowing it, the key question is whether you'll also claim it so that it stays a vital part of your remaining life's journey. While you may experience great clarity and deep awareness when you allow a why, embracing it in your life (the act of claiming) is critical if that why will serve you and walk with you on your journey.

For example, I experienced profound insights and clarity on the Camino through the whys of solitude, disconnection, pausing and letting go. However, if I didn't purposefully claim these whys in my continuing walk through life, then the impact of these whys would be relegated to moments and memories from the Camino. It's only when I claim them as ongoing whys that they become an integral part of my day-to-day life experiences. The great part is that it ultimately doesn't matter whether a why comes to you through claiming or allowing, but it does matter whether you choose to claim your whys, no matter what their origin.

> There's a funny thing about whys: sometimes we choose them, consciously and intentionally, and sometimes they choose us, if we're open to them.

There's a funny thing about whys: sometimes we choose them, consciously and intentionally, and sometimes they choose us, if we're open to them. Our whys serve us in so many beautiful ways. They compel us to keep going even when it's scary or hard. They help us carry on even when it's painful and uncertain. They allow us to move past and through obstacles and challenges in our life experiences. Your whys are at the heart of your ability and willingness to overcome whatever it is that you need to overcome. Your whys allow you to continue in pursuit of your dreams and goals no matter what events, circumstances or people seek to get in your way. My Camino whys allowed me to continue and finish the journey despite the painful injuries I'd experienced, and they were in many ways the wind beneath my wings that carried me along on the Camino.

Real Life Whys

It may be easy to connect with and understand the why concepts that I've shared from my Camino experience, but perhaps it's more difficult when it comes to everyday life. While the concepts are the same, I know that I didn't really understand the concept of why (and whys) until much later in my life. I grew up with a superficial understanding of whys. For example, when I was asked why I attended Ohio Northern University, I'd typically answer to play baseball. I also was used to being asked questions like "Why did you do that?" (often by my parents or a teacher). Another version was "Why would you do that?" (certainly no judgments in that question, right?). This same superficial and logical use of the word and concept of why carried into my professional career, and it wasn't until I was 36 years old that I started to experience and learn a different context for why – one that went deeper and was more about being intentional, purposeful and committed in my life and leadership.

In 1995, doctors discovered that my Dad had a serious brain tumor. It wasn't malignant, but it was very large and had to be removed. I even remember that the neurosurgeons' call with the news about the tumor came the day of my grandmother's funeral (my Mom's mom), and Mom was very upset about receiving this frightening news on the same day that we were burying her mom. The prognosis was fairly good, but there were no guarantees, and the surgery would be long and tedious. In fact, the surgery went longer than expected (thirteen hours), but after the surgery my Dad was okay. While he had several physical impacts from the brain surgery and was facing a significant recovery and rehabilitation process, he was committed to his recovery. I remember Dad whispering to me in the Intensive Care Recovery Room that he would soon be back to doing 100 push-ups a day. He ended up being in the hospital for thirty-nine days after the surgery.

Just Why

At that time, Dad was fifty-eight years old and was in very good shape. He worked out every day due to his role as the baseball coach at Wright State University, where he often made his much younger athletes shake their heads by doing the same workouts that he asked them to do. While Dad ended up with a couple of ongoing physical challenges from the surgery, he ultimately had close to a full recovery, and he did get back to his regimen of morning exercises and workouts. What I learned in watching Dad's recovery was the meaning and impact of a why. You might think that Dad's why for working hard was to recover physically, to get back to coaching, or to have a long and healthy life, etc. All good goals, but his true why (which he shared with me) was at the heart of his recovery. Dad's why and motivation was simple – to be around and able to play with his grandchildren. The eventual six grandchildren were still young in 1995, and several weren't yet born, but Dad was dedicated not only to being there, but being able to be physically active with his grandchildren. That was the why that made all the difference.

Since that time, I've come to better and more completely understand not only the meaning of whys, but their importance in helping me to live and lead in the ways that I desire. As I shared above regarding my Camino journey, there were whys that I claimed in advance, there were whys that showed up and which I allowed during the journey, and I then claimed many of those allowed whys after my return from Spain. There are also many different whys that come into play in every part of my life and leadership journey. Some of them flow from my personal mission:

I co-create a world of hope, safety and healing by modeling authenticity, vulnerability and unconditional love.

They're also evident through my core values: authenticity, vulnerability, integrity, full presence and unconditional love. Various other whys also come into play in big and small ways in both my personal and professional journey.

One of the key whys behind my business is the intention and commitment to help people and organizations get past the stories and beliefs that are keeping them from their goals, desires and impact. When you can truly connect to your whys, you can feel them – not just know them – and they'll have an emotional impact on you. I remember sitting on a couch being pushed by my marketing firm to answer this **question:** Why does what you do matter? I remember when I finally connected to the why (not just the logical reasons), and it came out of me something like this, with tears: *Because what I do is like breathing, and if I'm not doing this, I might as well not be alive.* Certainly not something that I'd thought or said before, and not something that I hear or say all the time, but it was real, deep and true – and this why feeds my passion for everything that I do in sharing a message of hope and healing to everyone that I speak to and coach. Quite literally, this big why takes my breath away when I consider its weight and possibilities.

Then there are smaller scale whys, such as the why behind choosing to mentor others beyond my coaching work. I'm currently mentoring ten men through an organization called the Mankind Project, and, while it requires a large investment of time, my why is to support other men and to pay it forward in developing the future leaders of this organization and the world. My why for often not making detailed plans when I travel is to keep myself open to all the possibilities and experiences that can unfold when I don't have a schedule. It's the why of adventure and synchronicity. My why for not booking reservations on the Camino was to allow my journey to be organic, rather than scripted, and to feed my desire for unexpected outcomes. My why for committing to a value of full presence is that I believe it's the greatest gift we can give to another human being. My whys (great and small, sometimes practical and sometimes philosophical) all help me to move through life with a greater sense of intention and purpose. They support me and even carry me through difficult times, and they allow me to live life with more passion and meaning – all great returns on the investment into creating and committing to whys throughout every part of my life.

What about your whys? Where have you claimed whys in your life? What whys are showing up as you allow them in? Think about it and, if you're willing, get crystal clear on the whys. For example, many of you will likely say that your children are your why, but what does that mean? What specifically is your why with respect to your children? If you think that your business is your why, what exactly is the why regarding your business? If you own a business, what's the why of your business? Your personal and business whys mean so much more than the whats. Similarly, what whys have been showing up in your life? Did you allow them, and have you now claimed them?

Keep in mind that size doesn't matter when it comes to whys. What matters most is the clarity of your whys, your commitment and dedication to your whys, and the intentions that you put behind your whys. The best way to know if your why is clear and real enough to you is to write it down or speak it to yourself. Do you feel it? Does it scare you? Does it bring up emotions in you? If you're ready, then take the steps now. Open yourself up to whys. Get crystal clear on your whys. And most important, embrace them, claim them and ignite them.

Keep in mind that size doesn't matter when it comes to whys. What matters most is the clarity of your whys, your commitment and dedication to your whys, and the intentions that you put behind your whys.

Why Whys

As we leave this consideration of the many different whys in your lives, it's important to consider the why of whys – in other words, why they matter and what value they'll add to your life's experiences and journey. In simplest terms, your whys are your secret weapon! Your whys are what will help you to build and sustain momentum. Your whys are the endless source of your passion. Your whys are your fuel and accelerant. Your whys are the means to your ends. Your whys are the ropes to help you overcome the obstacles that will inevitably show up on your journey. Your whys are what will smooth the road even in the midst of chaos and uncertainty. Your whys are the comfort and confidence you'll need no matter what doubts or setbacks you experience. Your whys are what will replace any need or desire for luck because your whys will help create synchronicities along the way.

If whys are the secret sauce, why are we hesitant to embrace our whys, both in claiming and allowing? There are several reasons. First, you may have grown up in an environment where whys weren't discussed or were even rejected. Perhaps people around you think that whys are extravagances and that the only thing that matters is keeping your head down and doing what you have to do to survive. In truth, whys are what allow you to shift from surviving to thriving. Second, some people believe that whys are only for certain people (e.g. people with more money, more success, more whatever). Third, some people (and perhaps you) believe that whys are just niceties and that they don't really matter. Finally, and often unconsciously, many falsely believe that they're not worthy of a why – that whys are only for those who have a grand plan to change the world. All of these beliefs are false and off-course. Whys are for everyone, and they come in all sizes. It's not the size of the why that matters, but rather the degree to which you claim it and thereby achieve all the gifts that flow from it.

As we wrap up this exploration of whys, I encourage you to keep these thoughts close to your heart. When in doubt, your why is the clarity! When you're struggling, your why is the inspiration! When you're uncertain or afraid, your why is the comfort! When you're confused, lost or hesitant, your why is the guide! When you're hurting and want to stop, your why is the relief! When you're in the dark, your why is one of the lights that will help guide you through the many challenges you'll face!

Your whys are the key to trusting that you and everything else will be okay. Your whys reassure you that you're already okay. Your whys are big enough to overcome any whats or hows. Your whys are the core ingredient that makes you unstoppable. Your whys are the answer that you've been searching for your entire life, and the deeper truth is that you've always had everything you needed. You've always had your whys locked inside of you, and once you've consciously chosen, intentionally committed to and openly embraced them (even the unexpected ones), you'll have armed yourself for whatever battles you're facing and equipped yourself for whatever journey you're taking. And your whys are just one step away! No matter what your challenges, remember the power, the wisdom and the inspiration of your whys, and when in doubt, Just Why on the road to your unstoppable you!

Chapter 12

Just Ask

*A*s children, we were all great and skilled at asking for what we wanted. I know that my two sons were never hesitant with the two words, "I want." Despite all our practice with asking for what we want as children, we quickly lose the ability and willingness to ask for what we want. I'm guessing that the answer for this is pretty simple – at some point, we decided that we weren't getting enough of what we asked for, we were experiencing negative reactions to our requests, and we started experiencing disappointment when we didn't get what we wanted. Another potential influence likely was hearing from others that asking for what you want is somehow selfish or arrogant (both "bad" things). I suspect that another contributor (indirectly) is the self-judgment that if we're not getting enough of what we asked for, then we must not deserve it. If you don't think you're worthy of having what you want, then you'll certainly be hesitant to ask for it. In order to minimize or eliminate these experiences, and especially if we don't think we're worthy of having what we want, we stop asking.

My Camino journey was filled with experiences around asking – two types of asking in particular – and both are key lessons to bring into your life. It certainly has transformed my life now to be more ready and willing to make these asks. The first is, as noted above, asking for what you want. The second and perhaps the most difficult is asking for the one thing that we can all use and need, but which we've been told (a cultural lie) is a last or never resort – asking for help or support. When I ask audiences if they think they're good at giving help and supporting others, nearly everyone's hands shoot up into the air. I get the same response when I ask about how open people are to being asked for help or support.

We're a culture of helpers that are slow (or even unwilling) to ask for or even to receive help.

However, the answer is vastly different when I ask how many people are good at asking for help. I'm lucky to see a handful of hands. For reasons we'll discuss in this chapter, we're a culture of helpers that are slow (or even unwilling) to ask for or even to receive help. This dichotomy gives us a heads up that shifting toward asking will have its challenges, so let's step into this world of asking – both asking for help and asking for what you want.

Even before I started on my Camino journey, I experienced the gift of receiving help because I had asked for it. I sought out a connection with Mark Leblanc and, while I invested in that coaching relationship through a donation, I also took the initiative to ask Mark to support me on my Camino adventure. I also regularly sought Mark out to ask him questions about planning and packing for the Camino. I experienced the same gift while on the Camino, since I regularly asked for help, whether it was for directions, for help with the language or to find a place to stay after the storm in O Cebreiro. I also asked clients to make accommodations in our working relationship to allow me to take the journey, while still meeting their expectations and needs. While this particular ask produced some fear, I asked anyway, in large part because of my Camino whys.

One of the most interesting experiences I had on the Camino related to a specific phrase that's become associated with the Camino. Actually, there are two of these special Camino phrases. The first is one that I heard and said to others many times every day: Buen Camino, which literally means "good road" in Spanish. However, on the Camino the phrase relates more to offering a fellow pilgrim a blessing of having a good journey or a good Camino experience. The other Camino phrase is much more limited in usage: Ultreia, which literally means "beyond" in

Latin. However, its Camino meaning goes much deeper and often refers to encouragement to keep going, to reach beyond what's easy and carry on. While I heard the phrase "buen camino" dozens of times every day (and spoke it just as often), I only heard the word ultreia one time on the Camino, and it was the time I needed to hear it the most.

It was my second day on the Camino, and I'd walked a long distance, fresh off the long and arduous walk on day one. As I neared what I hoped would be the end of the day, I was tired, sore and dehydrated (still learning my water lessons on the Camino), and hoping that the next turn would put me in the town of Samos. After walking alone for many hours and navigating through forests and countryside, I walked into a small village, hoping that I was nearing Samos. It was a warm day, and I was soaked through with sweat.

I saw a large group of people waiting to go into a church. After walking past the church, I discovered what they were all waiting for – a funeral procession drove past me on a small road. As I watched the procession go past me, I became deeply aware of my exhaustion and the pain in my feet. I was leaning heavily on my walking sticks when I heard a man shout, "Ultreia." I looked up to see him walking down the road to the funeral, and that was a special moment on the Camino. It was just what I needed to hear – a stranger apparently seeing me in distress and supporting me with that one encouraging word – keep going, onwards, carry on. That one word was the help that I needed in that moment, and while I didn't directly ask for it, perhaps I did – perhaps that man heard my plea for a dose of just a little more energy to keep going. That man and that word – ultreia – was one of the greatest gifts I was given on the Camino.

Asking for Help

Because I'd made the decision not to book lodging reservations on the Camino, there was one Spanish phrase that I learned well before I left: tienes una cama? Do you have a bed? I certainly asked this question many times when I walked into an albergue or hotel on the Camino. However, this question became nearly a plea for help when I finally arrived in the city of Portomarin, which is a decent-sized town on the Camino. It had been a long journey from Samos on my third day on the Camino, and I'd hoped to stop in the very small village of Morgade (a 13-plus mile day). I'd been walking that afternoon with Henry from Germany, and we both had planned to stay in Morgade that night. In fact, when we walked into Morgade (not much of a village really, more just a single albergue), I saw a couple of people that I'd briefly seen along the way. They were from the United States, and one of them was from Detroit. As I walked up, we exchanged greetings, and they asked if I wanted to join them in walking an additional 10 kilometers (approximately 6.2 miles) to Portomarin. I immediately said no. I was tired and sore, and the shin splints and painful feet issues were getting worse.

Just at that moment, Henry came out of the albergue, let me know that there was only one bed available and asked if I was okay with him taking it. I quickly agreed (Henry is older than me), and I was assured that I only had to walk another 1.5 miles to the next village, which had two albergues. I walked on and discovered that both of those albergues were already full, so I walked on and on and on.

Yes, you guessed it – I ended up walking all the way to Portomarin (a nearly 19-mile day) even though I was ready to rest after 13 miles. I made it to Portomarin for one simple reason – there was nowhere to stay and I didn't relish the idea of sleeping outside without a sleeping bag. After crossing a long bridge and river to the city of Portomarin, I was greeted with a very long and high set of stairs up into the city. Ugh, I thought, but I made it up the steps and up the ensuing hills to the center of town. However, I quickly found that there were few places to stay in Portomarin, and before long I'd asked my question – tienes una cama? – eleven times in this town of 1,500 people, and the answer had been no each time.

Finally, when I walked into albergue number twelve and was given another "no room at the inn" answer, I finally did it – I asked for help. *Me puedes ayudar* – Can you help me? Perhaps from a spirit of giving or perhaps because I looked so exhausted, the young woman made a phone call and then told me that there were beds available at another albergue several blocks away. I staggered into the very large building (120 bunk beds in a single room) and was thrilled to find a place to lay my head (albeit another top bunk, which seemed to be my lot on the Camino). It may seem like a small thing, but there was power in that moment of surrender and asking for help. I didn't think that I was so hesitant to ask for help, but I realized that I was deeply attached to doing things on my own.

This is one of the most important things that a leader can do with and for her or his team – to ask for help and thereby encourage the team to do likewise.

Somewhere in me was a story that if I had to ask for help about something so simple as finding a place to sleep, I was somehow inadequate or less than. The same is true for many of us when it comes to asking for help, but I've learned over the past few years that whether it's big help (dealing with a big life issue) or small help (asking for help in finding a bed to sleep in), asking for help is a sign and signal of strength. Rather than seeing and thinking of asking for help as a sign of weakness, more and more people are recognizing that asking for help is a sign of strength and, critically, that it encourages others to do the same. This is one of the most important things that a leader can do with and for her or his team – to ask for help and thereby encourage the team to do likewise.

Asking for What You Want

There's one universal truth that I've embraced about asking – if you don't ask for what you want, it's highly unlikely you'll get what you want. Well, you might want to talk back to me about luck, but luck is out of your control, and honestly I'm not a big believer in luck. Anyway, do you really want to live your life based upon the hope of luck? Actually, I know that some of you do want to live life based upon the hope for luck. I know this because you do it. It's also clear because you fail to ask for what you want, which is a signal of your reliance on luck. While we don't control much, giving your life and your outcomes over to luck involves the abdication of everything that you possess to help you influence your outcomes. As I shared above, it seems like there's a deeply held belief for some that asking for what you want is somehow arrogant or selfish.

While it certainly is self-focused, that's not necessarily the same as selfish, and, frankly, if you don't ask for what you want, then you're highly unlikely to get it. I also believe that failing to get clear on what you really want is another indirect way of avoiding asking for what you want. After all, you can't ask for what you want if you don't know what it is! Similarly, if you're not confident in your own worthiness of getting and achieving what you want, then you're very unlikely to ask for it. I often have people tell me that they don't ask for what they want because they probably won't get it, which is another way of abdicating to fate and the whims of others.

An even more interesting phenomenon is when people fail to ask for what they want, but then resent not getting what they wanted, even though they never asked for it. I continually encourage people to ask for what they want and also let them know that they might not get it. None of us are guaranteed anything, but I feel deeply that failing to ask for what I want is the surest way not to get what I want. And again, you must get clear on what you want in order to ask for it. Whether the ask is big or small, ask for what you want!

One of the best examples of asking for what you want shows up in some advice that I've been offering to others over the past few years, including to myself. Over the years, I've had many opportunities to coach, mentor or support people who are seeking to achieve something. Perhaps they're starting a new business, embarking on a new career, stepping into a new relationship or pursuing some other goal or objective. In the course of these discussions, I'm often asked for advice based upon my past experiences – some version of "What advice do you have for me?"

Several years ago, a friend of mine was taking the leap and starting his own consulting business, and we got together for drinks. At the end of the conversation, he asked me this **question:** "You've done this yourself and been doing this for some time. What's the best piece of advice you have to offer me?" I'd been asked this question many times before, but for the first time a new piece of advice came out of my mouth: Be Bold and Be Bold Sooner! I continued by encouraging him to trust himself and what he had to offer, and to do it more and sooner than he might think. To be bolder with everything, including his fees. To charge what he thought he was worth before he was certain. Essentially, to ask for what he wanted even if he didn't have the utmost confidence that he was worthy of it yet. While this advice came out unfiltered, it has become more defined and refined over the past few years, and my friend has shared with me how significantly this approach has enhanced his business. In short, he has been boldly asking for what he wants – and often getting it.

That's the thing about asking for what you want – you'll often get it, and what you get will often far outreach what you ever could have previously imagined. And it all starts with taking the bold steps to ask for what you want and to trust that you're worthy of it (even if you're not yet sure that you are). Asking for what you want is an act of vulnerability that pays off (not every time, of course, but most of the time), especially when you're clear on what you want and you're ready and willing to play your part in securing it.

> Asking for what you want is an act of vulnerability that pays off (not every time, of course, but most of the time), especially when you're clear on what you want and you're ready and willing to play your part in securing it.

I'm not suggesting that all you have to do is ask for what you want, lay in a hammock and wait for it to come. I'm talking about a co-creation that involves all of the things we're exploring in this book – working on yourself, honing your skills, enhancing your awareness, claiming your whys, setting clear intentions, pushing through your fears and taking action, all while asking for what you want. It's a collaboration of mind, body, soul and spirit, and you're at the center of it all. If you're uncomfortable being the co-creator of your own life and outcomes, then sit back, keep your fingers crossed and live with the results. If, instead, you're ready to be the co-creator of your life and outcomes, then grab onto the wheel, take your foot off the brake, put your foot down on the accelerator, point yourself down the road of your choosing, ask for what you want, and put your car into drive. This is the essence of any journey, but you don't have to do it alone – that's where asking for help and support become important.

What Do You Want?

What are you waiting for? Do you know what you want? Are you ready and willing to ask for it? Dump that old story that failing to ask for what you want is somehow humble. Rather, failing to ask for what you want is more about fear and doubt than humility. What do you want in your relationships, career, business, family and friends? Are you clear?

If you're willing to be clear (which itself takes courage), what does it look like to ask for what you want? In some cases, it's obvious – it's just a matter of saying the words. In other cases, it may be subtler, and it will take some discernment to determine in what ways you can ask for what you want.

One truth about asking for what you want is this – asking for what you want is an act of worthiness, which is why we often come up short in it. In fact, the idea that asking for what you want is somehow selfish can be a way of masking worthiness questions in the failure to ask. Let's be clear about this – ask for what you want, but not because you're sure to get it. Even if you're not sure, ask for what you want because you trust that you deserve it. Even if you don't get it, that doesn't mean you don't deserve it – it only means that you didn't get it *yet*. You don't control what you get, but you do control what you ask for, and only you can ask for what you want. No one else can ask for you because the trust behind the ask must come through and from you.

Are you ready to have what you desire and deserve? Are you ready to co-create new outcomes in every part of your life? Are you ready to leap and to be bold? Are you ready and willing to be clear – which we often fail to do? If your answer is yes, then take the step, trust yourself and *Just Ask*!

Chapter 13

Just Keep Going

*Y*ou already know about the various painful physical challenges that I faced throughout the Camino. While these challenges were very real, they also opened the door to a number of rich experiences and deep learnings. One of the biggest came near the very end of my travels in Spain as I was waiting for my flight back home from Madrid. I'd completed my Camino journey, made my way back to Madrid, and had gotten a wonderful night's sleep in a comfortable hotel bed. Although I was rested, my feet were still hurting terribly, and I went outside on a beautiful early June afternoon to get some sunshine and to journal about my experiences. That day I experienced a powerful lesson from a man I never met nor exchanged a word with.

I was wearing flip-flops, and I found some cool, soft grass where I could sit down in the sun. I was enjoying a celebratory cigar, capturing my thoughts and feelings in my journal, and simply enjoying being off my feet. Even when I was sitting, both feet were still hurting, and this wish popped into my head: "I so wish my feet weren't hurting so badly." As I uttered this wish, I looked up and saw a man making his way down the sidewalk in front of me to the bus stop. That's when I "met" my teacher. He was the only person on the sidewalk at that moment, and he stood out because he was walking on crutches *because he was missing his left leg.*

When I looked up and saw him, this thought went through my mind: "I'll bet he would love to have a left leg that was in pain." Here I was complaining about the pain in my feet and legs, and this man was living with no leg. In that moment, I looked up and said "Thank you." Thank you for the wake-up call. Thank you for the lesson. Thank you for the perspective. Thank you for the reminder. My feet were still hurting, but instead of focusing on the pain and what I wished was gone, I shifted to gratitude to have my feet, to have been able to take and complete my journey, and to be sitting in the grass in Madrid enjoying the sunshine. It's yet another example of the many ways that the Camino worked in and through me during my journey.

That man was meant to be my teacher that sunny afternoon in Madrid, and I'm grateful for the lesson and for the awareness. I brought that perspective and awareness back with me from the Camino, and I offer it now to you. Do with it as you please, but my hope is that you'll keep this powerful lesson in mind – a gift from a stranger walking through my life – as you read and experience this book.

Where are you doing something similar in your life? Where are you focusing on what you don't have or what's not working, while failing to see the blessings that exist in the midst of it all? Are you so focused on your own issues, challenges and perhaps even pain that you're failing to see and support those around you who are facing their own issues and pain? I was gifted with a jolt of awareness by a man who never knew me or even saw me, but that's the way that gifts work *if you're open to see them.*

Whether I was hot and tired, or wet and exhausted, or feeling the pain in my feet and ankles, these all take on new meaning when you're taking a journey that involves nothing but walking across northern Spain. While I somehow had it in my head that the Camino was relatively flat, it turned out that there were more elevation changes than I'd expected. Although there weren't too many big elevation changes and climbs (other than on my first day), there were ample ups and downs on the Camino. This included what can appear to be very large hills to ascend and descend, as well as long stretches of path or road ahead of you. While you often can't see what's ahead of you, there are places on the Camino where you can see quite some distance down the road, and those distances are exaggerated when you're tired and hurting. It was these very hills and distances that taught me a very critical lesson that transcends the Camino into my life – a lesson that will also help you not only to navigate life differently, but to achieve more with less stress and disappointment. Interested in that?

This unexpected lesson can best be summarized in these few contrarian words of wisdom – *keep your eyes OFF the goal*. I know, I know – you've likely been told your entire life that it's vital to always keep your eyes ON the goal. I was told and thought the same thing, but the Camino taught me a different lesson – a lesson that's transforming my outcomes and, most important, my experience towards those outcomes. It's a lesson about where you focus – and where you don't. It's a lesson about inspiring you to go forward rather than discouraging you due to a lack of progress. It's a lesson about the vital importance of setting yourself up for success with bite-sized short-term goals, even if it's just walking a few feet down the road. And, it's a lesson about one of the most important needs on any pursuit or journey – momentum. Join me as we take this vital journey into a new way of living and leading towards your goals and objectives based upon one simple truth – *just keep going*.

Take Your Eyes Off the Goal

I get it – keeping your eyes on the goal (or on the prize, as the saying goes) seems to make sense, and it's certainly a perspective that has been engrained in me most of my life. After all, don't you have to keep your focus on the goal to get there? That's what I thought for a long time, but I've now discovered that it's not true – it's a false and misleading approach to achieving new outcomes. What I learned on the Camino is that even if I take my eyes off the goal, I'll still get there as long as I trust my direction and just keep going. Yes, be clear on your direction and occasionally look up and assess *whether your objective still fits and feels right*, but there's no need to regularly look at the goal or

What I learned on the Camino is that even if I take my eyes off the goal, I'll still get there as long as I trust my direction and just keep going.

objective. While you might occasionally get off course, you'll still achieve the objective, with just as much certainty of the outcome and with so much less stress and disappointment.

I can clearly remember the precise moment when this lesson hit me on the Camino. My feet were hurting, and I was traveling through a small village, taking different twists and turns, which is a typical Camino experience. When I reached the outskirts of the village, I turned to my left (the direction I was heading) and saw a very long stretch of road in front of me that seemed to go miles into the distance, finally disappearing over a small ridge and into a forest. While I'm sure that the distance was shorter than it seemed, the distance was exaggerated by my exhaustion and pain. It also didn't help that I didn't see anyone on the road, feeding a sense of aloneness and making the distance seem even further. However, just as I did many times every day, I just started walking down that road in the direction of my goal.

After walking what turned out to be (but didn't feel like) a short distance, I looked up to see how far I'd gone, and all I could see was the long road left ahead of me. While I was slightly closer, the end of the road seemed so far away – as if I'd barely traveled any distance – and I felt so discouraged. It was as if I was walking in slow motion or my steps were only a quarter of their actual length. I'd thought I was making good progress, but looking up to see my goal (the end of the road I could see) had left me feeling let down, and I had to encourage myself to push on.

I continued to have this same experience during my walk down that long road – I'd walk what I thought was a good distance, only to look up and see how much further I still had to go. Over and over I made the same mistake of looking up, only to continually feel discouraged and wonder if I'd ever get to the end of that road. That's when it hit me – *I need to stop looking at the end of the road*. Looking at the end of the road wasn't inspiring me; it was discouraging me. It wasn't helping me; it was hindering me. Focusing on the end of the road wasn't pushing me forward; it was actually pushing me back. So I made a decision to stop looking at the end of the road, not only on this road but on every road and path I'd travel for the rest of my Camino journey. I'd do the same thing – taking my eyes OFF the goal – when it came to going up or down (which actually hurt more than going up) a large hill.

One thing I learned a great deal about on the Camino was the concept of false summits, a common experience when hiking or walking. A false summit is when it appears that you're making the journey to the top of a particular hill, only to discover at "the top" that there's another hill or climb right after it. This happened so many times on the Camino and was intensely discouraging, especially when my focus was on what I thought was the end, and then I realized that what I thought was the end or outcome didn't matter. All that matters is arriving at whatever the end or outcome is, and it doesn't matter if I know when that end is about to occur. Rather, I'll know it when I get there.

While this was an important awareness and lesson, turning the thought into action was much more challenging than I expected. Despite my decision to keep my eyes off the goal, I found myself continually drawn to look up and at the goal, which took me out of the present. Instead of just being in the moment of moving forward one step at a time, I was drawn to where I was going (in the future) and to what was coming (rather than where I already was). Something in my prior life training kept telling me to look up and see my goal, and nearly every time the experience was the same – disappointment and discouragement. Only on those rare occasions when I'd look up and I was actually at my goal did I feel some sense of accomplishment.

I wasn't feeling much accomplishment the rest of the time I was walking because my attention was focused on the end goal, not all the mini-goals along the way and certainly not the simple act of continuing to take just one step at a time. After all, those single steps were the only path to my objective, and the same is true for every goal or outcome you're seeking in your personal or professional life. While having the goals is great, there's always only one way to achieve them, and that's one step at a time.

I realized that something inside of me desperately wanted and needed to know how far I'd come and, more importantly, how close I was to my goal. I learned on the Camino and now deeply embrace the truth that I don't need to know how far I've gone or how much further I have to go – I just have to be committed to the outcome and keep moving – just one step at a time. On the Camino, though, this

need to know was so great that I had to force myself not to look up, but as I created this new way of being (not looking up), my Camino experience changed. I was still tired, and my feet still hurt, but whenever I kept my eyes on the short-term goals (just one step at a time), I experienced very little disappointment or discouragement. Not surprisingly, I still achieved those larger objectives (the end of long road, the ultimate top of a hill or arriving at the next village where I could rest) without keeping my

This new practice also allowed me to have deeper and more present experiences on the Camino since my focus had shifted from where I was going to two simple realities – where I was, and just keep moving.

eyes on the goal. This new journey also had very little discouragement from not getting where I wanted to be fast enough.

By the end of my Camino journey, I'd fundamentally changed my approach to goals, and I rarely looked up. Rather, I was focused on just going and taking in all the sights, sounds and experiences that were all around me and right in front of me. This new practice also allowed me to have deeper and more present experiences on the Camino since my focus had shifted from where I was going to two simple realities – where I was, and just keep moving.

I've now brought this new mindset and approach into my personal and professional life and, like it did for the Camino, it has transformed my life experience by minimizing stress and discouragement, enhancing my journey, increasing my success in achieving my objectives and, in many cases, actually accelerating my path to my desired outcomes. It may sound crazy, especially since this mindset is so fundamentally different from what I was (and most of us are) used to, but it just makes sense. You can get to wherever you want to go if you just get clear on your objective and desired outcome, set some strong short-term goals that will keep you on track and motivated, and just keep going. Imagine as we continue on this journey the ways that this different approach can help you get where you want to go, consistently and predictably, while at the same time minimizing stress and discouragement.

Set Short-Term Goals

While you may all realize the importance of short-term goals – literally, next actions, analogous to something like a sprint rather than a marathon – it became very real for me on the Camino. Combining short-term goals with the idea of keeping your eyes OFF the long-term goal will enhance your journey and your achievements. Despite the simplicity and obvious need for short-term goals, my experience is that most of us personally and professionally are failing to set them. We either embark in pursuit of a journey with no long-term or short-term goals at all – simply starting – or we set the long-term goals without taking the time to create the short-term goals that are required to get us to the objective.

Think about the last time you sought to lose weight. You probably set a goal of losing a certain amount of weight or inches by some date far down the road. This is the nature of new year's resolutions – I'll lose weight this year (a terrible goal because it's too vague), I'll lose 25 pounds (without setting a time by which that goal should be achieved), or I'll lose 25 pounds by June 30th (a long-term goal, but with no short-term steps). Yes, having the long-term goals is important, but it's even more vital to have short-term goals (e.g. a certain number of pounds every week) and action items (e.g. exercise a certain number of times a week, establish actionable changes in your diet, etc.).

When I lost 40 pounds a couple of years ago, people continually asked me how I did it, and I told them it was simple. First, I set a long-term goal for the first six months of twenty pounds. Second, I set a weekly exercise goal of at least three times a week of thirty minutes of cardio. Third, I used an app on my phone to track my daily calories against a daily goal. When I look back at my weight loss journey, I achieved the outcome (first losing the 20 pounds, and then setting another goal to lose an additional 20 pounds) by setting short term goals, committing to them and actually doing them. I never focused on the long-term weight loss goals because they were largely irrelevant – they were just markers of some outcome down the road. All that mattered was having and achieving the very small goals every week, which meant doing the even smaller things every day.

On the Camino, my goals were even smaller and simpler. Yes, I had some longer goals during a day, but my short-term goals were often nothing more than reaching an oil mark on the road or a certain fence post. The pain in my feet was so extreme that I had to find short-term goals that provided me with constant successes, and once I achieved them I'd immediately set another short-term goal. Most important, every single short-term goal was supported and achieved by the smallest of next actions – just one step – and these single steps, the setting of very short-term goals and my achievement of them (even if small), created a powerful outcome not only for my Camino journey, but in pursuing any objective in life – the power of momentum.

Momentum Is Real

I've often thought about the importance of momentum, but it was only on the Camino that I really came to understand it – how to create it, and the various impacts and gifts that momentum delivers. Whether you're embarking on a Camino or a different journey, any pursuit of an objective requires momentum to help you achieve your desired outcomes.

Let's first look at some of these vital outcomes that momentum delivers, which I experienced the truth of on the Camino. One of the biggest gifts of momentum is that it makes your journey easier and acts as a lubricant on any pursuit. Lao Tzu is widely quoted as follows: "A journey of a thousand miles begins with one step." This is certainly a practical truth, and it was an important truth for me on the Camino, but the key is that the single step must be followed by another step, and another step, and another step. And once you create some rhythm of steps, you've achieved the amazing power of momentum.

Imagine what my Camino journey would have been like if I took one step, paused, took another step, paused, took another step, etc. Not only would my journey have taken much longer, but I may not have ever completed any part of it. When I'm only taking one step at a time and not building any momentum, then every step requires more work and effort.

This is why momentum not only makes the journey easier, but acts like a lubricant taking us more swiftly and predictably towards our outcomes.

The next gift of momentum is the role it plays to help you overcome the natural occurrences of fatigue and discouragement. When I'm limited to single steps without momentum, it's easier for discouragement and setbacks to cause me to doubt, delay or even fail to start. Momentum doesn't prevent exhaustion, frustration and discouragement, but it's a powerful tool in overcoming them.

Similarly, momentum is vital when you face the inevitable obstacles and challenges along the way, whatever they may be. Momentum is the thing that keeps us moving over, around and sometimes through our obstacles and challenges. I've always been drawn to the metaphor of the stream and the stone, including this quote from H. Jackson Brown, Jr.: "In the confrontation between the stream and the rock, the stream always wins – not through strength but by perseverance." While I still find this perspective helpful, it struck me that it's only focused on the ultimate outcome – that the stream will eventually wear down and wash away the rock. However, what happens when the stream initially confronts the rock? The stream doesn't stop, and it certainly doesn't think about ways past the rock – it just keeps moving and *it finds a way around the rock.* The same is true for momentum in your life. When you're able to create momentum, it helps sustain itself and you on your journey, which helps keep you moving despite any obstacles.

When you're able to create momentum, it helps sustain itself and you on your journey, which helps keep you moving despite any obstacles.

Not only does momentum help you navigate past or through obstacles, it helps to smooth out the inevitable bumps and rough spots. If you're very slowly making your way as you pursue some objective, you'll feel and perhaps be slowed by the bumps and rough spots. However, when you're able to achieve some level of momentum, the bumps are just bumps and the momentum will carry you over them with less effort and minimal delay. In short, momentum is like a rubber raft that carries you and speeds you on your journey.

Thus, momentum is essential and it's always and only achieved in one way – not by big action or giant steps, but by small actions and little steps taken continually towards your desired outcomes. Even better, you don't have to plan for or design momentum – it's a natural outcome and occurrence of taking one step followed by another and another, all while you continue to *just keep going.*

Look Back

One unexpected Camino gift and lesson was the importance of periodically looking back along your journey. While it's easy to keep your eyes focused on what's ahead of you, I found great gifts and perspectives in occasionally turning around to look back on the Camino (and now in my life's journey). I remember one particular moment early on the Camino where I turned around and experienced a completely different perspective (a different view), and this led me to continue this practice throughout my journey. While I loved seeing where I was going, seeing the different view of where I'd been was an important part of my experience.

Looking back also allowed me to embrace and celebrate, even if in small ways, what I'd accomplished. It's so much easier and more typical to continually focus on the distance left to travel, without acknowledging the distance you've already covered. I vividly remember the different feeling I had when looking ahead and seeing how far I still had to go versus looking back and celebrating how far I'd come. This is so true in your life as well. We're constantly looking ahead to what we've not yet achieved, but we rarely take time to turn around, look back and allow ourselves to feel good about the road we've already traveled.

Yes, keep reaching for that which you desire in your personal or professional life, and set those big hairy audacious goals, but always remember to look back, acknowledge what you've already done and achieved, and celebrate the journey you've already made. Life is made up of one journey after another, and each leg of each journey is worthy of celebration and even a giant pat on the back. Look at you and all that you've already achieved! There's more for you in the future to achieve, but make sure you remember to look back and bless yourself for the journey you've already taken.

Your Journey

The Camino was my journey and was only one of the many journeys I've taken thus far in my life, and there are more journeys left to take, experience and complete. What about your journeys, objectives and desired outcomes? What are you seeking to achieve in your business or career? What different experience do you desire from and in your relationships? What I learned on the Camino is that any goal or objective is really a journey – a journey that will be filled with highs and lows, obstacles and challenges, bumps and bruises, failures and successes, setbacks and accelerations. I also now deeply understand that every journey is made up of individual experiences that are just as important as (and often more important than) the journey itself, and the same is true for every journey you've taken, are taking and will take in the future.

I'd love to be able to assure you that you will achieve every objective and outcome you desire, but that would be naïve and misleading. What I do know is that there are different ways of pursuing your objectives that will always shift your experiences and thus will often shift your outcomes. The shifts shared in this chapter were learned through difficult times on my Camino journey, and I've brought them back into my personal and business journey. I now understand that I don't have to keep my eyes on the goal and that, in fact, my chances of achieving my objectives are better served by keeping my eyes off the goal. I now know that the key to my dreams is focusing on the short-term goals and even just next actions (the next steps), committing to them and sustaining them long enough to create the magic of momentum. I also now understand and embrace the truth that I only control one thing – myself – which means that I control my next steps, which will empower me for every pursuit and journey the rest of my life.

If you want to improve a relationship, focus on small acts that will build the relationship. If you want to improve your sales, focus on the small and perhaps different actions you can take today. If you want to change your financial situation, commit to making different financial choices every day. If you want to take a trip, focus on small steps that will make that trip a reality at some point down the road. Set your long-term goals, and then take your eyes off them. Set your short-term goals and keep your eyes on those. Identify the small steps that will get you where you want to go, and then take them. Take the small steps even when it's scary, difficult or even painful. Trust yourself even in the face of challenges. Commit to the steps long enough to build momentum and then just keep going.

Keep your eyes off the long-term goal, focus on the short-term goals (next actions) and commit to the next step.

As you move forward in every part of your life, I encourage you to dump the old perspectives about goals. Keep your eyes off the long-term goal, focus on the short-term goals (next actions) and commit to the next step. Embrace the power of momentum and know that you create momentum through the simplest acts of taking one step at a time followed by another and another. Your desired goals, outcomes and life are at the end of the road, and you may not be able to see them, but if you want them enough to take just one step and then another you'll be on the road to those desires. Expect setback and obstacles. Expect even that it may be painful at times. But know that you've what it takes to get there if you *Just Keep Going*!

Chapter 14

Just Walk Backwards

I'm a huge fan of *Seinfeld* – the show about nothing – and I'm convinced that everything you need to know about life, relationships and leadership can be found there. However, you may have to look at things differently in order to find what you should do amidst the many examples in *Seinfeld* of what NOT to do. One particularly memorable episode is called "The Opposite" and involves George's decision to do the exact opposite of what he would normally do. George takes his first step into the opposite when he approaches a beautiful woman in the diner and says the following:

> "My name is George. I'm unemployed,
> and I live with my parents."

To George's surprise, she's impressed and agrees to date him, and George continues his strategy of opposite actions throughout the episode (at least until it inevitably blows up on him). While I always laughed at this concept – doing the opposite – I never imagined how insightful and even profound it was until I took my Camino journey.

One thing I painfully learned on the Camino is that having injured feet and ankles is no fun and presents many genuine physical challenges. I also learned that while walking uphill with bad feet and ankles was challenging, it paled in comparison to the pain I experienced when I had to walk downhill. While walking uphill puts stress on your heart (through exertion) and your calves and other muscles, walking downhill puts extra stress and strain on your hips, knees, shins, ankles and feet. This was not good news when I had painful issues on both feet and a shin splint on both ankles, and I made various attempts to find a solution.

I tried walking slower and walking faster. I tried leaning back into the hill and leaning over towards the downhill. I also tried running downhill, which mainly increased the pain but at least made the downhill journey quicker. I also noticed that some Camino pilgrims were zig-zagging down the hills, which reduced some of the stress on my feet and ankles, but it wasn't a full solution. Nothing I tried worked, and I was getting desperate to find a way to reduce the pain I was experiencing. They say that desperate times call for desperate measures and that desperation can fuel innovation, and this proved to be the case for me on the Camino. When nothing else worked or helped I tried something radical – perhaps even crazy – and began to walk the downhills *backward*.

If you're puzzled, it's okay. It's normal – many people are confused when I talk to them about walking backwards on the Camino. Yes, I'm literally talking about turning full around, facing up the hill and walking down the hill backwards. And here's the amazing part – it worked. While it didn't eliminate the pain, walking backwards greatly reduced the pain I was experiencing, and for my last seven days on the Camino I walked downhill backwards nearly seventy percent of the time. In fact, I walked downhill backwards every time unless the hill was too treacherous to navigate backwards (e.g. because of large boulders, excessive ruts or other obstacles). Even if the trail was rocky, I still walked backwards down the hill to experience the relief in my feet and ankles, as well as to speed up my pace – most of the time I could walk backwards down the hill faster than I could walk it facing forward.

You might be wondering if I walked backwards over rocks and

streams, and the answer is yes. Yes, I walked backward on flat surfaces, bumpy surfaces and rocky surfaces. Yes, I wasn't looking where I was going, since walking with my head turned over my shoulder was even more difficult. I developed a little strategy where I'd take and count one hundred steps, glance over my shoulder to see what the terrain looked like "behind me," and then face uphill again and keep walking backwards.

Incredibly, I never fell and only stumbled once or twice when I stepped on an unexpected or unusually shaped rock or root. I pretty quickly developed the ability to walk backwards very fast, and in several places I was rocketing down the hill backwards while swinging my walking sticks in my arms. I often wondered what I looked like flying down a hill walking backwards with my arms and walking sticks swinging back and forth, and I'm sure that I made some impression on everyone who witnessed this strategy in action.

Not only did I walk backwards, but I noticed that other people started doing the same – mimicking my bizarre walking approach and continuing it once they discovered that it worked. Trust me, I saw the "you're crazy" looks from many people, especially when I passed them walking backwards and facing them. A popular greeting on the Camino is to wish everyone that you pass (99% of all pilgrims are walking the same direction – west) "Buen Camino" – have a good Camino journey. You walk past them, and as you do you look over your shoulder and wish them "Buen Camino." Imagine their surprise when they were walking downhill facing forward and I would come walking past them backwards and facing up the hill, look them in the eye and say, "Buen Camino" as I continued down the hill! I swear that some people were so confused that they wondered if they were facing the wrong direction.

Even when I talked about my unique strategy in the evenings, I was met with great resistance from other pilgrims, and I heard all of these comments:

"I couldn't do that."
"I wouldn't be able to maintain my balance."
"I'd be falling all the time."

The funny thing is that I thought about all of these things too, but I did it anyway, and it turns out that I was wrong. And I discovered that

if you're not getting the results you want in any aspect of your life or leadership, are you doing things just a little differ- ent or are you radically shifting your perspec- tives and actions?

I was wrong – that I could walk backwards – only when I chose to take the risk and try it – daring to do something different in order to change the outcomes and pain that I was experiencing. What's the old saying – insan- ity is doing the same thing over and over and hoping for a different result? I decided not to be insane and to instead do something differ- ent – to invoke the wisdom of taking a risk by engaging in what I like to call crazy normal. Crazy normal is where other people think you're crazy, but your choices and actions are actually normal and logical when you consider what you're facing. I now embrace crazy normal as one of my life and leadership mantras, and walking backwards is one of my crazy normal practices.

My question to you is simple – if you're not getting the results you want in any aspect of your life or leadership, are you doing things just a little different or are you radically shifting your perspectives and actions? Maybe it's time to *Just Walk Backwards*.

Why Walk Backwards?

Before I dive into the various practical ways that walking backwards will serve you, let's first look at some obvious benefits of this shift. As noted above, walking backwards is one antidote for the insanity that many of us engage in every day – doing the same things over and over and hoping for different outcomes. As for me, hope isn't a strategy, and it's not some- thing I want to pin my future on. While I believe in hope (the belief that things can and will change), I choose not to lean on hope as my strategy and tactics.

Another reality of change is that if you're stuck or otherwise in a rut of any kind, you can't get out of it with slight adjustments and small turns (like zigzagging your way down a hill). While you may be able to move out in small steps and actions (just one step at a time), you often need to make extreme shifts and adjustments to escape the rut. After all, if you're in a rut in a car, you can't get out of the rut with slight turns of the wheel and at low speeds. Instead, you've got to make hard turns and accelerate at the same time. Walking backwards is a similar example of this approach.

Whether you're ready to embrace this truth or not, slight changes and course adjustments are often not enough to change your path and outcomes. In more and more cases I encounter, radical shifts are required, especially when the prior patterns, practices and processes have been long standing and engrained. While it may feel scary, real change often requires bold action and sometimes this means doing the opposite and walking backwards.

We all know that over time we develop certain patterns, habits and muscles (i.e. ways of doing things), and when you attempt to change them it can be uncomfortable and perhaps even painful. I've learned this over the years with my daily routine of push-ups. In the beginning, I did traditional push-ups every day, and my muscles adjusted to that form. However, when I started doing push-ups using the "perfect push-up" rotating tool, the push-ups were harder because I was using different muscles. Then, a couple of years ago, I decided to start doing diamond push-ups, where you put your hands together in a diamond shape in the center of your body and press up and down from that position. These push-ups are generally regarded as more difficult, and I felt they were for some time. However, when I now do traditional push-ups, they're more difficult than the diamonds because my muscles have adapted to the diamond push-ups.

The same is true with the ways that you live, relate and lead. Over time, you quickly develop comfort zones and muscle memory that make what you've always done (and the ways you've always done it) easier and more comfortable. However, we also know that over time what you've always done will inevitably either cease to work or become less effective than you need it to be. That's why change is always necessary at some point and why it's critical for you to be willing to stretch yourself and your muscles in different directions, and sometimes that means doing the opposite. It may feel odd and uncomfortable, but that just means that you're exercising a new muscle and trying something new. Allow yourself to feel odd and uncomfortable and take the risk of walking backwards – it may be just what you need to change everything in your experiences and outcomes.

Walking Backwards in Life

It's fairly easily to understand what it means to walk backwards on the downhills of the Camino, but understanding the ways to implement walking backwards in your day-to-day living and leading can be more challenging. Shortly after I returned from my Camino journey, a good friend of mine called me and asked if I could stop by that evening for a chat. I agreed, and he quickly shared with me that he had a very real challenge with his romantic relationship. He was heading out of town for a trip and really wanted to talk to his partner about how he was feeling about several recent events before he left. However, all of their recent conversations hadn't gone well, and he was struggling to find a way to talk to his partner in a way that would work. After asking a few more questions, he clarified that he wanted to express to his partner how he was feeling about a couple of things, and he indicated that she hadn't been very receptive to this type of sharing. That's when I said, "Well, maybe it's time to walk backwards."

In response to his expected question of what that meant, I said something like the following:

> We know that you sharing your feelings with your partner about certain things that she's done isn't working. While I certainly believe that your feelings are important and worthy of sharing, that approach is clearly not working. What if, instead of telling your partner how you feel, you went home and simply asked your partner how she's feeling about things?

He noted that he should be able to share his feelings, and I agreed, but he also agreed that him sharing his feelings wasn't moving the communication or the relationship forward at that time. So, he agreed to try the opposite – to walk backwards – and he headed home to try a different approach.

A couple of days later my friend called me back with an update. As planned, he'd gone home and, rather than sharing what he needed to share, asked his partner how she was feeling about things. In response, she began to share more than she'd been sharing previously, and he just listened. While he still wanted to share, he walked backwards and just held space open for her feelings. At the end of what he termed one of their best conversations in months, she thanked him and said that this was the first time that she'd felt heard in months.

This was only the beginning, as their communication began to improve steadily from there. A short time later, he was able to share his feelings, which was the original starting point for our conversation, and their overall communication began improving. While certainly many factors were at work, walking backwards by doing the opposite of what he'd done before opened the door to different and deeper communication and sharing.

After returning from my Camino journey, I discovered that I'm not the first to contemplate this concept of walking backwards. I was reading Mark Manson's book *The Subtle Art of Not Giving a F*ck: A Counterintuitive Approach to Living a Good Life* (2016), and much of his book and its philosophies are based upon the concept of living and thinking counterintuitively. In the book, Manson references the work of two influential philosophical writers, Aldous Huxley and Alan Watts. Huxley and Watts offered what they

The more conscious our efforts towards better results are, the more likely it is that our results will diminish.

called the law of reversed effort, which in simple terms translates roughly to: the harder we try, the less we succeed (aka the "backwards law"). A slightly more complex explanation of this phenomenon is that the more conscious our efforts towards better results are, the more likely it is that our results will diminish.

Here's what Aldous Huxley had to say about the backwards law:

"The harder we try with the conscious will to do something, the less we shall succeed. Proficiency and the results of proficiency come only to those who have learned the *paradoxical art of doing and not doing,* or combining relaxation with activity, of letting go as a person in order that the immanent and transcendent unknown quantity may take hold. We cannot make ourselves understand; the most we can do is to foster a state of mind, in which understanding may come to us."

In very simple terms, Alan Watts offered this truth: "Muddy water is best cleared by leaving it alone."

Essentially, Watts and Huxley both suggested that the harder you try, the less success you'll have. Obviously, this is the opposite of what most of us have been taught throughout our lives. If you're like me, you were told that you must always try harder and seek to do your best. While this seems to make sense, their backwards law makes just as much (if not more) sense. If you always try harder, there will be an inevitable point of diminishing returns that you hit *because of this continual and persistent effort.* What Watts and Huxley discovered is that optimal performance requires a mix of effort and relaxation because if you don't have the combination of both you'll wear out the machine (i.e. you) with and through your efforts.

Their backwards law tells us that at various points we need to back off from our efforts in order to achieve the most optimal results. While walking backwards and the backwards law aren't precisely aligned, the foundation is the same – we often need to do the opposite of what we've always thought, believed and done in order to overcome and achieve.

A former educator shared with me another real-life example of the impact of walking backwards when it comes to working with students. She described a former student as a "selective mute" who hadn't spoken in nearly ten years. Whenever they had read aloud sessions, she routinely encouraged this student to give it a try, told him he was respected and cared for and had his classmates quietly cheer him on, etc. None of these typical efforts worked, so she decided to skip over him in the rotation and to leave it alone from that point on. In other words, she did the opposite.

After a few weeks of just greeting him with a smile and sending him off the same way, but never asking him to participate, a wonderful thing happened. They were doing a read aloud session in a giant circle, and his classmates knew to skip over him. On that very special day, as the reader to his right began the passage, suddenly there were two voices; the second belonged to the selective mute student! In her estimation, this walking backward experience brought about one of the greatest moments of her career.

Here are some other examples that people have shared with me of walking backward in everyday life:

In the 12-Step recovery context, there's often a discussion of taking "contrary action" – doing the opposite of what your addiction tells you to do.

You have a daunting task or project to accomplish, and you're doubting your abilities to complete it, or you're intimidated by it. The old thought might be to escape, delay or avoid it. The walking backwards approach is to call a friend, tell them about the resistance or fear and ask for support so that you can push back the obstacles and do the task.

A dear friend of mine contracted a disease that caused her to lose her speech. After thirty-eight years of marriage, she and her husband found a new way to communicate using sign language and a boogie board.

In parenting, when your kids need you to engage the most, they often act out the most. The typical response is to let their behavior push you away until they're ready to act better, but instead you do the opposite and give them even more positive attention.

When a friend is venting about the same ongoing problem and you want to give them advice that they haven't asked for, I've found that giving that intended advice to myself has been invaluable and has taken me out of judging my friend.

The key is to catch yourself doing what you've always done or what seems natural, and to instead try something that seems a bit crazy and is often the complete opposite of what you're thinking or doing. This may seem risky, but if what you're already doing isn't working, then why not?

Another everyday example of walking backwards is making the shift from statements, telling and advice to questions. While it may seem like a small thing, statements (telling) and questions (asking) are opposites. Telling is what you do when you share what you think and believe in order to attempt to educate or convince someone else. Questions are the opposite and are designed to elicit what the other person thinks and believes in order to educate yourself and to better understand. Much like other forms of walking backwards, the shift from statements to questions will require you to use different muscles and will therefore be uncomfortable. It also requires you to let go of controlling and demanding and instead seek to understand. Rather than giving advice based upon what you think, questions are the best way to help someone find their own answers, awareness and insight. This is what leaders do, and it requires that you walk backwards with questions.

Walking backwards is often required in order to inspire and fuel innovation. While many innovations present themselves as adjustments to what already is, the path to those innovations often demands that we do the opposite in order to create the shifts that feed the innovation. One example is the old saying that "the customer is always right." For decades, this concept was interpreted to mean that businesses and their employees always had to agree with customers, which included being subjected to verbal and sometimes even physical harassment and abuse. Today, however, many businesses are doing the opposite and putting their values ahead of their customers. Perhaps you've heard about the Alamo Drafthouse Cinemas which are now across the country. The Alamo Drafthouse holds and promotes a Code of Conduct, which includes the following:

Respect. Find out what it means to us.

At Alamo Drafthouse we respect our guests, our employees, and the work of the filmmakers that unspools on screen. That's why...

- We have a Code of Conduct that strictly prohibits harassment of any type by anyone at our theater.
- We have zero tolerance for talking or using a cell phone of any kind during films. *We'll kick you out, promise. We've got backup.*
- We don't allow anyone under the age of 18 to see a film unaccompanied unless they're part of our Victory Vanguard program.
- To minimize distractions, we generally don't admit infants and small children. We do, however, offer weekly daytime screenings under the banner of Alamo for All, meant for young families and guests with special needs.
- We don't show paid advertisements on our screens. Instead, if you arrive early you'll see a custom preshow our video squad has filled with content we think you'll love.

What? That's not what everyone else is doing in the movie industry! Alamo Drafthouse has now become famous for kicking customers out for violating their policies, including for texting during a movie. While a small percentage of people are outraged, the vast majority of people are applauding the Alamo Drafthouse for taking a stand to protect the experience of the rest of the customers. This walking backwards is helping the Alamo Drafthouse not only to stand out, but to excel and succeed.

Think about other examples of walking backwards, including innovations across every industry over the decades. Imagine sitting in the room when the people at 3M talked about the idea of turning their failing adhesive product into what we now know as sticky notes. Imagine the many conversations inside Apple when they were ideating the next new technology innovation. Nelson Mandela was famously quoted as saying, "It always seems impossible *until it's done*," and the generations have been transformed by women and men who walked backwards in order to turn the impossible into the possible.

When everyone else was honoring the laws of the land regarding African Americans and relegating themselves to the back of the bus, Rosa Parks boldly chose to walk backwards and sit in the whites only section of the bus. Similarly, and looking back to Nelson Mandela, when he was released from prison most people were urging him to exact vengeance on those that had imprisoned him. Instead, Mandela walked and talked a message of forgiveness and reconciliation – walking backwards.

In history, imagine being part of the 20th Maine under the command of Colonel Joshua Lawrence Chamberlain on Little Round Top at Gettysburg. The 20th Maine was the far left end of the Union line, was outnumbered and had been told that they had to hold the line at all costs. When the 20th Maine was virtually out of ammunition, Colonel Chamberlain issued the now famous order to "fix bayonets" and to charge down the hill. Can you imagine the responses of some of Chamberlain's men? What the hell are you talking about – we have no ammunition – but this version of walking backwards had a significant impact on the battle and may have saved the Union army that day. Certainly, Chamberlain's order was the opposite of what many other leaders would have done.

Our lives and indeed our world have been continuously and repeatedly transformed for thousands of years by men, women and groups who were willing to do things differently – often the opposite – by walking backwards. Where are you dabbling around the edges hoping to change things and outcomes, but finding that the changes are too small or the edges not sharp enough? Where are you hesitating to walk backwards in your business, relationships, families and communities? More importantly, are you ready – are you ready to take the risk, to be bold, to do the opposite, to walk backwards?

Now is the time for radical shifts, dramatically different thinking and, most important, bold and courageous action to change things for the better and the different. Do you hear this call in your organization, with your team, in your life, with your relationships or in your family? And will you heed this call and step differently – to turn around and even walk backwards to be the change you wish to see in the world? Make no mistake that people are waiting for someone to change things – will you be the one to walk backwards?

An Unexpected Gift of Walking Backwards

I remember the first moment when I turned around to walk backwards. I was trying something new with one purpose – to help ease my pain and allow me to navigate my Camino journey – but I experienced something completely new and unexpected. I found that when I dared to turn around to walk backwards I was able to see two things – two things that didn't exist as long as I was walking forwards.

First, I was able to see where I'd come from and appreciate how far I'd come. I still had many miles to go, but it felt good to bless and acknowledge what I'd already accomplished. Do you do the same in your life or with your team? Do you look back and allow yourself to just be grateful for the progress you've made – for the many miles you've already traveled and survived? Life goes on, and the challenges and opportunities will always be ahead of us. Even though we may always be striving to take our next steps (whether in business, community, relationships or life), it's worth taking time to turn around and see and bless the road you've already traveled. Walking backwards is one way to give yourself the gift of looking back and honoring all that you already are and have achieved.

Second, turning around to walk backwards offers us a unique perspective. While the future is always uncertain, when you turn around and look back you'll see a perspective that's different than any that you've ever seen before. Here's the key – we often spend too much time looking back, but it's only a problem when we look back to judge and criticize ourselves and others. Looking back isn't the problem as long as we don't linger, and we can look back while we keep moving forward by walking backwards. Life is full, but we can only see the fullness when we're willing to look back and take in the view of all that has been. They say that our lives flash before our eyes when we have a life-or-death experience, but why wait?

Why wait for our lives to be threatened or lost before we see our lives like a movie? Walking backwards offers you the gift of experiencing and witnessing your life (the ups and downs, the successes and failures and, most important, the lessons learned) while still moving forward. That's one hell of a return on the simple act of turning around to walk backwards.

Ready to Get Naked?

Sorry to disappoint you, but there are no naked pictures in this book. However, in writing this book I've come to realize one key thing relating to walking backwards – it's an act of vulnerability. When you walk backwards, you're exposed. You can't see everything that's coming to trip you up, and you may fall (often). If you try to walk backwards while keeping your head turned over your shoulder to see where you're going,

I've come to realize one key thing relating to walking backwards - it's an act of vulnerability.

you'll never get anywhere. It's too slow and too safe. When you walk backwards, you won't be able to see everything or anticipate every challenge, risk or setback. Much like my Camino journey walking backwards downhill, you have to just cut loose, swing your hips and walking sticks, and trust. There it is – walking backwards requires trust in yourself and in the world. You have to trust that everything including you will be okay, even if you stumble or fall. Are you willing to get naked, to trust, to stumble, to fall, to get dirty?

When I was walking backwards on the Camino, it was more about survival than anything else – surviving the pain of my feet and ankles. But I've learned the deeper lessons of walking backwards since my return from the Camino. I've learned that many people are actually waiting for someone to walk backwards – to change things, to make a difference.

I don't have eyes in the back of my head, but somehow for all the miles I walked backwards, downhill, on the Camino, I never fell down. Somehow I was okay. Somehow everything worked out. And somehow and somewhere in all of the necessity of walking backwards, I learned ways to live and lead differently in every part of my life. The Camino humbled me and schooled me. The Camino taught me and taunted me. The Camino shoved me and kicked me. The Camino was outside me, and it was (and remains) inside me.

Are you ready to get naked? Are you ready to change things? Are you ready to be a person of impact? Are you ready to make a difference? The path is clear, even if uncertain. All you have to do is *Just Walk Backwards!*

Chapter 15

Just Be Present

*A*s I write this chapter, I'm scared and uncertain. Will it make sense? Will you understand? Will you trust me enough to be open? Will you be able to follow the bread crumbs I offer to living a life in the present? Will it be enough? Will I be enough? I'd love to tell you that I don't have these doubts, but I'm human. Without knowing it, I unconsciously kept putting off this chapter – this epic chapter – until the end. About halfway through writing this book, I realized I was putting off this chapter, and then I embraced that truth. I let myself be okay with saving this chapter for last. I let avoiding my fears be okay for a time, so long as I eventually stepped into my fears and shared with you the deepest truth that I can imagine – presence is the answer to everything. Presence is the answer to fear, to pain, to doubt, to shame, to relationship, to uncertainty, to change, to connection, to joy! I guess that's what scared me so much – knowing the truth about presence and wondering if I'm worthy to share this truth with you. Even more important, can I share it in ways that allow you to find your own way back to the present?

I woke up in a hotel in Raleigh, NC, and watched a movie. Little did I know that this "wake up" would lead to a journey to Spain and the Camino, and little did I know that it would all lead me *back to the present and back to me*. Little did I know that the Camino would change everything for me and, more important, allow me to learn and grow enough to share this journey with you – and hopefully, to give you these keys for your own journey. As I said at the beginning, you don't have to travel to Spain and walk the Camino. You don't have to live and experience my experience. But you do have to choose – choose to be awake, choose to risk, choose to be vulnerable, choose to love, choose to care, choose to shift, choose to walk your road, choose your journey.

Presence is a journey, but it's not a journey forward. It's a journey back to the present.

One of the most surprising clarities I've discovered on these journeys – the Camino journey, my life journey and this book journey – is that presence is a journey, but it's not a journey forward. It's a journey *back to the present*. In the beginning – your beginning and my beginning at our births – we came into the world fully in the present. I read some time ago that for unknown reasons we're born with only two natural fears – fear of falling (perhaps from being bounced around and carried in the womb hanging two feet off the ground) and fear of loud noises. The rest of our fears are "gifted" to us through our life experiences and the people in our lives. We're taught to be afraid and, similarly, we're taught not to be present.

When we're born, we only care about the present (the moment). If we're tired, we sleep. We don't think about being tired or wanting to sleep, we just do it. If we're hungry, we cry for food. It's not a thought process, and we don't wonder if there will be enough food. We cry out and we get food. However, if there's no food, then we unconsciously start to form beliefs about the existence of and access to food. Similarly, babies aren't afraid. They might be startled, but they're not consciously afraid because they don't know how to be afraid. They're living in the moment.

When we're born, we don't think about what happened yesterday or what might happen tomorrow, and we don't think about what the people we're with are thinking about us. When a baby wets or soils its diaper, it doesn't get embarrassed and worry what others will think. It just did what it needed and wanted to do in the moment. All of this is to say that presence isn't something you search for and move towards, but rather something that you journey back to in order to live your life with a mind-set and experience like that of a child.

Now that we've established that our path to the present is a journey back, let's further explore the gifts of presence that the Camino offered me and now offers you. As I shared earlier, there were so many amazing synchronicities on my journey, and some of them directly related to presence. In the year leading up to my Camino journey, I'd experienced a great deal of what I call aloneness. I didn't feel lonely, but I felt alone despite having many, many people in my life. I often called this experience "feeling alone in the crowd." As I explored this phenomenon, I realized that it was part of my journey of growth and life.

In fact, one of my several leadership mentors (Phil Beverly) and I had many conversations about this reality – aloneness – and the fact that this experience was likely a necessary part of my life and leadership journey. They often say leadership can feel lonely, and I was having that precise experience in every part of my life. This included the truth that as we grow there's a significant risk that we'll lose people and relationships in our life. It's not something we consciously do, but rather a natural outcome of any journey of awakening and consciousness. If you want to grow, you must be willing to risk these types of losses in your life.

The Camino was indeed a journey of aloneness, solitude and presence. While there were plenty of people that I met on the Camino, I walked most of the journey alone. Yes, I shared a dinner table with other pilgrims many evenings and struck up conversations, and I also had several synchronistic experiences of running into people I'd met on the Camino, but I mostly walked alone.

I quickly discovered that many Camino pilgrims created traveling groups – people who met and effectively decided to travel together. They would often walk together during the day, but even if not, they made advance arrangements to connect back up in the next town for dinner. On my first day, upon hearing about this group dynamic, I was initially drawn to it because it felt good to think that I'd be with people that I knew, even if I'd just met them. However, on day one I realized that this wasn't what I wanted, and I even (again, unconsciously) walked at a pace and distance that moved me away from nearly everyone that I had met. I realized that most days I was walking just a little further than the typical Camino traveler would walk, and I'd end up at the next town, city or village beyond where most of the people I met during the day would have stopped. Without knowing it or intending it, I was creating a journey of solitude on the Camino – not knowing that this unconscious choice would be at the heart of my Camino journey and its lessons.

I'd also made a decision ahead of time to be fully in the present during my journey by not listening to any music or books along the way. While I saw many Camino pilgrims with earbuds, I walked without any extraneous distractions or inputs other than whatever the Camino had to offer me – sights, sounds, smells, touches and people. While all of this didn't ensure that my Camino journey would be lived fully in the present, everything was set up (both with and without intention) to allow me to live this journey in the present. And this was a profound gift of the Camino.

While there are many ways to experience the Camino, its core for me is about presence. It's easier there than in my everyday life to find and live in the present. The essence of the Camino is presence, and I know that most of my journey was walked, lived and experienced in the present. While the painful issues in my feet were certainly challenges to staying in the present, living in presence was one key element of my ability to continue and fully experience the Camino despite these issues. In the end, the Camino wasn't a lonely journey, but it was an alonely journey – a journey in and ultimately into the present because upon returning, I discovered a transformational level of presence in my life.

Prior to leaving for Spain, I would have described my personal level of presence and groundedness this way – I felt like my feet were firmly grounded on the earth. Solid. Balanced. Here. Upon my return, however, there'd been an incredible deepening in all of these. No longer did I feel merely grounded to the earth, but I felt like there was a large steel rod that ran from inside me to the center of the earth. I shared with friends that I felt like a thousand people could try to push me over at once, but they wouldn't be able to move me, and I wouldn't need to offer any resistance. It was the most unique (and now continuing, when I stay present) feeling of peace, balance and groundedness I could ever imagine. It was the feeling of being unstoppable, and each one of you can experience life this same way – unstoppable – when you find your way back to the present and choose to live your life here and now.

> It was the feeling of being unstoppable, and each one of you can experience life this same way - unstoppable - when you find your way back to the present and choose to live your life here and now.

What's Presence?

Within a week of returning from my Camino journey, I was led to a book by Amy Cuddy called *Presence: Bringing Your Boldest Self to Your Biggest Challenges* (2015), and this book expanded and transformed my comprehension and experience of presence in my life. Previously, I had limited my commitment to and experience of presence to personal interactions – in other words, being fully present when I'm with other people. While this is a key element of presence, I took away a wider view of presence from Amy Cuddy and her book, including this summary conclusion: *The degree of your presence (experienced by others) is determined by your degree of presence (living in the state of presence).* Wow – if you want to have a great presence, you must be more present, which essentially means that you're willing to trust your most authentic self as enough and offer all of you to every situation, person and experience.

Cuddy writes in *Presence*, "The authentic self is an experience — a state, not a trait." (page 43). She goes on to share the following:

> "Your authentic best self — your boldest self — isn't about psyching yourself up or saying, 'I'm the best at this task' or 'I'm a winner.' Your boldest self emerges through the experience of having full access to your values, traits, and strengths and knowing that you can autonomously and sincerely express them through your actions and interactions" (51).

Cuddy summarizes as follows: "In short: the manifest qualities of presence - confidence, enthusiasm, comfort, being captivating - are taken as signs of authenticity, and for good reason – the more we're able to be ourselves, the more we're able to be present. And that makes us convincing" (29).

Here's the real power and empowerment of presence: "But what matters more is that [presence] will allow you to approach stressful situations without anxiety, fear and dread, and to leave [you] without regret, doubt and frustration" (*Presence*, 25-26). As for the ways you present yourself with others when you're present, Cuddy says it simply: "Presence manifests as confidence without arrogance" (34). In what ways would your life and leadership be different if you were more consistently showing up with others in this form of presence? In what ways would your impact grow and accelerate if people most often experienced you as confident, enthusiastic, authentic and without arrogance? However, achieving this form of presence will certainly require you to be authentic and vulnerable.

"If you're protecting yourself against harm—emotional harm or humiliation—you can't be present, because you're too protected" (*Presence*, 63). In summarizing her thoughts on presence and the source of presence within ourselves, Cuddy quotes Walt Whitman: "We convince by our presence, and to convince others we need to convince ourselves" (41). In other words, presence is ultimately an inside job, which creates profound shifts in our impact and influence with everyone, everything and every experience.

One other thing to keep in mind about presence – it isn't necessarily an every moment thing. While I've made great strides in the quantity and depth of my presence, I have my moments when I'm not in the moment, not present. The question isn't whether you can achieve full-time, 24 / 7 presence, but whether you're willing to do the inside work to put down your old beliefs, stories and insecurities in order to move towards a life lived more authentically and more in the present.

As Amy Cuddy confirms, "Presence, as I mean it throughout these pages, is the state of being attuned to and able to comfortably express our true thoughts, feelings, values, and potential. That's it. It isn't a permanent, transcendent mode of being. It comes and goes. It is a moment-to-moment phenomenon" (*Presence*, 24). To be clear, the journey back to the present never ends – it's a daily commitment and way of living that must be continually reaffirmed through awareness and practice.

With this foundation in mind, let's now look at some clear examples of what it means to *not be present*:

- Participating in a job interview and wondering what the interviewer is thinking about your responses.
- Participating in a sales meeting and wondering what the prospect is thinking about your answers.
- Unwillingness to make eye contact with others.
- Talking fast and being unwilling to pause or uncomfortable with pausing.
- Experiencing fear – because fear relates to what might happen in the future.
- Experiencing anger – because anger relates to what happened in the past.
- Any thoughts of insecurity or questioning your worthiness – because they're based upon past self-judgments and self-perceptions.
- Engaging in a conversation and thinking about something that happened in the past (even if 10 minutes ago) or something you have to do in the future.
- Listening to someone else speak while thinking about what you'll say in response.

I could go on and on with examples, but the point is that when you're present everything about you is here and now, allowing you to experience the moment without trying to figure out what people are thinking, especially about you.

> Presence is the most powerful state of being on the planet – it's the secret sauce – and presence is the only state of being that allows you to experience being unstoppable.

What I really want you to know is that presence is the most powerful state of being on the planet – it's the secret sauce – and presence is the only state of being that allows you to experience being unstoppable. And make no mistake – you can't become more vulnerable, authentic and self-trusting by being present; *you become more present when you're vulnerable, authentic and self-trusting.* That's why the journey to presence is indeed a journey back to the essence of you – the unspoiled, untainted and healthy you.

If you're not already convinced that presence is the answer AND that it's worth pursuing for your own life and leadership journey, then here's what you must know: presence isn't only a gift, presence is THE GIFT. It's a gift you give yourself based upon the differences it will make in your own life experience – no fear, no stress, no doubts, deeper and more intimate relationships, being unstoppable. How's that for a gift to yourself? Even more important, presence is a gift that you give to everyone that experiences your presence because when you're present you give another person the most powerful and loving gift there is to offer – the experience of being the most important person in the world in that moment. Are you ready to be the gift for yourself? Are you ready to give the gift of presence to others? Continue with me on this journey as we find our way back to the present.

Obstacles to Presence

While the gifts of presence are clear, the journey to presence will have several obstacles to overcome, and these are five of the most daunting:

- Nearly all of us have grown up and lived an experience of not being present, which means that we must change our stories, beliefs and habits to being present.
- Our culture today is designed for anything but presence, including the role of ready access to distracting technology.
- In order to get back to presence, you must also make the journey back through, around and past your various self-doubts and insecurities.
- Your presence will be limited by your selfish nature.
- In order to be present, you must be vulnerable.

While these obstacles are very real, they can be overcome – sometimes slowly and in small steps, and sometimes in giant leaps of self-awareness. Every small step will help to accelerate your journey to fuller and deeper presence.

In confronting these obstacles to presence, let's start with what's likely the biggest one – the self-doubts, insecurities and self-limiting stories and beliefs that form the foundation of who we *think we are and what we think we're capable of being and achieving*. I could spend dozens of chapters on this journey and, in fact, my second book was entirely dedicated to it: *Unmask: Let Go of Who You're "Supposed" to Be & Unleash Your True Leader* (Motivational Press 2014). In *Unmask* I shared much of my own personal journey up to that time and offered tools and shifts to help you move past your old stories (the process of debunking those stories) in order to live and lead from your most authentic self. In short, you must debunk and unwrite your old self-limiting stories and gradually rewrite your own self-stories in order to find your way back to presence. As Amy Cuddy shares, "Presence stems from believing our own stories," which in this context refers to your new stories based upon a fundamental belief that you're good enough, worthy and powerful. I encourage you to seek out and read *Unmask*, since it will give you more than enough tools to help you navigate this critical obstacle to presence.

The next obstacle to presence is related to the first, but it's also based upon the habit of non-presence that you learned through the voices and actions of others from the moment you were born. As noted above, we learned to be afraid and to have self-doubts. While it's easy to blame our lack of presence on a distracted and distracting culture (see below), the truth is that we've been creating a distracted culture and distracted personal interactions for decades. When were we most present – before or after the invention of these now "old" technologies – the telephone, the radio and the television? While the cell phone and now smart phones moved us further away from presence, that habit had already been started by the various forms of technology already available.

We also have been practicing non-present habits in our business dealings for decades. Think about where you sit when you're meeting someone in a restaurant or coffee shop. Are you facing the door where you can see everyone that comes in and who else might be there, or are you willing to have your back to the door and focus on the person you're with? When you're out networking in business, are you fully focused on the person you're with, or are you keeping your eyes open to scan for other people you might see or run into? What did you see practiced in your home when it came to being fully present and listening to others? Did your parents model presence and intentional listening or distracted listening and perhaps hearing what's said in conversations without really investing in the person they were listening to? How long have you been told or shown that multi-tasking (not being present to one thing at a time) is the way to do and achieve more? Essentially, most of us have been injected with non-presence for most of our existence, and thus getting back to presence will require that you put away old and deeply ingrained ways of thinking, living, communicating and relating.

Next, we come to perhaps the most obvious obstacle to presence today – our smart phones. How often do we see friends or family sitting together somewhere, and every person has their face buried in their phone? Perhaps this is your standard mode of interaction with others. Even if you think this isn't who you are, think again: I often hear people tell me how frustrated they are with people not being present, while they're some of the most non-present people I know. In other words, the absence of presence can be a huge blind spot for many of us. We're now so far removed from being present that presence is even uncomfortable. I regularly have people tell me that my presence – with my eyes, my attention, my intention, my commitment and my energy – is too intense to handle. We now have a culture where presence is experienced as something foreign and uncomfortable. Talk about a large obstacle to overcome!

Finally, we come to the obstacle of selfishness, which I'm guessing you'll reject as not true about you, but I hope you'll hang with me and be open to seeing the ways that our own selfishness gets in the way of our presence. First, let's be clear on what it means to be selfish or self-focused – most fundamentally, it's simply whenever your focus is on yourself. I'm not saying that this is always a bad thing, but it can be an obstacle to presence.

Here are a number of examples of ways that we're selfish or overly self-focused that prevent us from being present:

- Sitting with someone in public while keeping your eye on who else is there so that you can say hello to them *is about you.*
- "Listening" to someone talk while working on what you'll say in response *is about you.*
- Keeping your eyes and ears open for the next text or email on your phone *is about you.*
- Talking over someone *is about you.*
- Inserting yourself into someone else's story (e.g. someone tells you a story about them, and you have to tell them about your "similar" story) *is about you.*
- Monopolizing a conversation *is about you.*
- Telling people what to do *is about you.*
- Talking fast and not pausing *is about you.*
- Wondering what people think about you or what you say *is about you.*
- Convincing yourself that you can multi-task and that multi-tasking is more productive when all the research says otherwise *is about you.*

Okay, enough ... I'll stop there. Hopefully, you get the point. Here's a simple way to rephrase this concept – if you want to be present for others, you have to make everything about others. Unless and until you're willing to get yourself and your wants out of the way, you won't be able to give and receive this most amazing gift of presence.

> Unless and until you're willing to get yourself and your wants out of the way, you won't be able to give and receive this most amazing gift of presence.

Now we come to an unexpected and very large obstacle to presence – in order to be present with someone else, you must be willing to be vulnerable. This is a particularly challenging obstacle to presence because so many of us resist and even reject the idea of being vulnerable with another person. However, if you want to be more present, you must be willing to be more vulnerable.

Recently, I was talking with a leadership mentee of mine, and she indicated that she has a strong desire to be more present with others, but she found that she was consistently struggling with being present, despite her wants. As we talked through this unknown obstacle, it struck me that one of her deepest fears is being vulnerable with another person. When I checked with her about the ways that her lack of vulnerability gets in the way of her being present, she immediately connected the dots and said that it was a big factor. Here's what I took away from that conversation – if you're fully present for another person, it creates a safe space for that person to be vulnerable, and that allows you to really see this now vulnerable person. However, it makes perfect logical sense that in order to experience someone else being vulnerable, I must also be vulnerable first.

Wow – I didn't see this truth coming, but I've since given it much thought and shared the concept with many others, and everything continues to confirm the proposition that presence requires vulnerability. After all, vulnerability includes the willingness to let others really see who you are (the real you), and this would of course be a key element in creating a present experience for someone else so that they can share who they are with you.

If you're starting to see the ways that your vulnerability directly impacts your presence, then you're well on your way to being more present. Hopefully, you're also seeing the ways that being present (giving the gift of presence) opens the door to more authentic and intimate conversations, connections and relationships, as well as enhancing the depth of your sharing, learning and collaboration. While you may be uncomfortable being vulnerable, that will be an obstacle you must overcome in order to give the gift of presence to others and to reap the rewards in your own journey from your own enhanced presence.

Yes, there are and always will be obstacles to presence, but they can be diminished and overcome, and the next section will give you tools for overcoming the obstacles and getting back to (and maintaining) your presence. If you're on board and committed, let's continue together the journey to your present and unstoppable you.

Getting Present (and Staying There)

Ultimately, the best path back to the present is to move past the obstacles to presence discussed above. However, we still need some tools to get present in the moment and then to stay there. What follows are a couple of tangible tactics that will serve you well on your journey to the present, as well as a shift around commitment that will help you not only get present but stay present.

The first presence tool is the simplest, yet it requires you to be aware enough to know that you need to do it. All you need to do is take a breath. Yes, simply take a breath. I know you all think that you take breaths every day, but the breathing you do all day is just surviving. You breathe and take breaths without thinking about it – it's automatic – but taking a purposeful and conscious breath requires that you slow down (and even stop) in the moment to take that breath. The reason this works is that in order to take a purposeful and intentional breath, you must be present, **and** the act of taking that breath is an action in the present moment. When you're taking a conscious breath, you're in the present. It really is that simple, yet deeply spiritual and profound.

Author and mindfulness thought leader Thich Nhat Hanh offers this regarding conscious breathing:

> "The way we start producing the medicine of mindfulness is by stopping and taking a conscious breath, giving our complete attention [presence] to our in-breath and our out-breath."

(*No Mud, No Lotus*, Parallax Press 2014, 18). In directly connecting the dots between breathing and presence, Hanh goes on to write: "To take one mindful breath requires the presence of our mind, our body, and our intention" (23). Thus, conscious breaths are a key element for finding your way back to the present.

The other presence tool can be done alone or in conjunction with the purposeful breath discussed above, and it requires that you do just one thing – ask yourself this **question:** Am I present? In order to ask yourself this question, you must be nearly present and, when you ask yourself the question, you immediately become present. Even if you weren't present before the question, the asking of the question brings you immediately back to the present. You don't really even have to think about the answer because the mere question puts you in the present.

There you have it – two simple tools (a conscious breath and the question, "Am I present?") that are guaranteed to bring you to the present. Now the trick is to find a way to stay there for more than just that minor moment. The answer is really no trick at all, but rather a commitment – a commitment you can make both generally and, in each moment, and to every person that you're interacting with.

The first step of the presence commitment is to make a global commitment to be present in every part of your life, whether it's in one-on-one interactions, group gatherings, when traveling or when participating in a particular task or project. While a commitment alone will not ensure that you'll live and relate in the present, it will go a long way towards orienting you towards presence. In addition, when you're committed to being present, it's much more difficult for distractions to take you out of the present. A big part of this is that once you make a commitment, your integrity is on the line. In other words, when you're committed to being present, the internal drive of your integrity kicks into gear, helps you find your way to presence and keeps you there.

Let me be clear about the nature of this commitment to presence – it must be a real commitment. Vague statements you say to yourself or others such as "I'd like to be more present" or "I wish I was more present" are not commitments. These are merely aspirations, and as such they have very little impact on being more present. If they did, we'd all be living and leading more often in the present because there's certainly no shortage of people saying that they would "like to be more present." Commitment means commitment – being clear with yourself and everyone around you that you're committed to being present. This opens the door to your own enhanced presence and invites others around you to help you find the present and stay there.

If you've committed to others to be more present, also give them permission to (and, in fact, request that they) tell you when they perceive that you're not being present. Knowing how difficult it often is for people to share difficult things with us, especially in the workplace, I suggest you arm the people around you with a simple phrase to bring the question of presence to the table. In fact, a simple question is the answer when it comes to presence. Let everyone around you know that they're welcomed to ask you this question at any time: "Are you present?" As you already know from above, when you're asked that question (by yourself or someone else), it immediately brings you to the present. It also allows you to be more aware of when you've not been present and to assess the obstacles to presence that you're experiencing. Other people can help you grow more into the present, but it first requires that you make the outward commitment to presence and ask to be held accountable to that commitment.

Other people can help you grow more into the present, but it first requires that you make the outward commitment to presence and ask to be held accountable to that commitment.

In addition to making a general commitment to presence, your journey to presence will be greatly enhanced and accelerated when you make specific presence commitments with the people around you. When you're about to have an interaction of any kind with someone, tell them (and thereby yourself as well) that you're committed to being present while you're together. Once you make such a commitment, it's much more difficult to fail to be present with them.

You can do the same thing in the moments when you're not able to be present but want to be present for someone in a future conversation or interaction. Take a look at this example:

Other Person: Do you have a few minutes to talk about the project?

You: Right now I'm not able to be present with you; however, I want to be fully present for this conversation. Can we talk in thirty minutes, and I'll be present with you then?

Rather than pretending to be present or attempting to multi-task your way through the conversation, you stay present to whatever you're currently doing or working on (and thus are more productive). You also make a commitment to be present with and for this person when you have the later conversation as agreed. Thus, you set yourself up to be present with this person when you're later together. You've now told yourself that you're committed to being present, and you've made the same commitment to them, for which they can hold you accountable.

There you have it – three simple tools to help you to live and lead in the present. First, take a conscious breath. Second, ask yourself the question, Am I present? Third, commit to being present, both generally and in particular interactions. When you infuse your life and leadership with these presence tools, you'll find that presence will become more and more your every day and every moment experience. As a result, you'll more often and more fully experience all the gifts of presence, which I'll walk through later in this chapter.

Sharp Edges of Presence

Among the many challenges of living in the present is that it's so easy to wrongly believe that we're present, and many of us have a false belief that we're more present than we actually are. The reality of the present is that it's a very sharp edge – you're either present or you're not present. You're not mostly present or sort of present – you are or are not. We also misunderstand the present, which keeps us from getting there, staying there and living there.

Presence has been described in so many different ways and phrases, including the following:

Be Here Now
Be Where You Are

Just Be Present

Stay Where Your Feet Are
Here Now
In the Moment

They sound great, but what do they mean? Despite the challenges of being present, presence itself is simple – it means you're fully here, right now in this moment. This means you're not thinking about other things, other places, other people or other to-dos. It means that you're fully with and attentive to whomever and whatever is front of you, whether it's a person, a task or a project. It means that you're all in.

This doesn't mean you don't have other thoughts, just that you're not allowing your thoughts to interfere with what or who's in front of you. For example, I often get ideas when I'm with someone else in a conversation. The act of having the idea (whether related to them or not) doesn't take me out of the present, but it quickly can if I allow myself to focus on that idea rather than the person or project in front of me. In order to stay present, I take a moment to jot down the idea for me to think about later. If I'm with someone at the time, I'll ask them for a brief moment to write the idea down, and I'll often tell them, "I want to write down this idea so that I can stay present with you." If I continue to think about the idea or try to make sure that I remember it, then I'm not present with the person I'm with.

Similarly, when you're talking to someone, you'll have many thoughts, memories or feelings. Perhaps you'll be reminded of another person, event or experience in your life, and you may choose to share that with the person you're with. You may also choose not to share it and, instead, let it go so that you can stay present. You may "think" that having other thoughts isn't a distraction from the present (because you're a master multi-tasker), but when you're with those other thoughts, you're not with the person in front of you.

The same happens when you're working on a project – instead of being present with the task or project, you're present with the other thoughts which take you away from whatever is in front of you. As noted above, presence is a sharp edge – you're either present or not – and your presence can quickly shift and change. The question isn't whether you'll be drawn out of the present, but whether you'll be aware enough to quickly release the non-present thoughts in order to get back to the present.

Another way we're often not present is a bit tricky, and you'll likely recognize it immediately. When you're wondering what others are thinking about you and the things you're saying, you're not present. Two obvious examples are job interviews and sales meetings. If you're wondering about or trying to figure out what the interviewer or potential client is thinking about what you've just said, then you're not present, and this means that you're also not fully listening. Rather than being fully attentive to the other person, you're self-focused, and this isn't present. You may have heard the suggestion that you just focus on being you or that you need only to be you, and this is just a different way of encouraging you to be present. When you're you – fully you – you're present, trusting that who you are and what you say is enough.

One of the easiest ways to know if you're present or not is to be alert for time traveling, because there's no time travel in the present.

One of the easiest ways to know if you're present or not is to be alert for time traveling, because there's no time travel in the present. What's time travel? Let's look at several examples that occur when you're not present. Think about the times that you're worrying or stressing about something that happened in the past, whether big or small, recently or many years ago. All of those things you worry about occurred outside the present, and being in the present eliminates stress, worry and regrets.

The worries of the past can't co-exist with the present. If you're worrying about the mistake you made yesterday at work, you're not present. If you're thinking about the disagreement you had with your partner last week, you're not present. If you're feeling bad about forgetting to call your mother on her birthday, you're not present. Not only are you not present when you're time traveling to the past, you're not serving yourself either since these negative thoughts about past events don't move you forward. Instead, they keep you in the past rather than the present.

"But what about 'positive' thoughts about the past?" you say. The answer is that carrying over so-called positive thoughts about the past also keeps you from being present. This is neither good nor bad, but not being present is still not being present, and living in the past will still keep you from the gifts of the present. For example, think about how distracted you are after coming back from vacation when you spend your time thinking about the amazing experiences. Yes, they're great memories, but they'll keep you from being your most effective and impactful in your present work. These great memories will also keep you from being present with another person. You're with someone for some purpose, personal or professional, but you're thinking about your recent vacation and you're not fully present and listening. If you want to share your experiences with that person, then share them – sharing them is part of the present; however, thinking about them instead of being present is time traveling.

Another example of time traveling is anger. We like to think that being angry is an act of the present, but only the anger is happening in the present – it doesn't exist in the present. If I lost you, then stick with me a moment longer. I recently had this discussion (aka disagreement) with a coaching client who insisted that his anger was part of being present … until I asked him these questions:

Me: What are you angry about?
Client: Something that someone failed to do.
Me: When did they fail to do it?
Client: Yesterday.
Me: See, time travel. You're angry about something that happened yesterday, which means that you're not present. You were angry in that moment, but it was based on something that happened the day before. You weren't dealing with the issue, just being angry about it.

Are you with me? Anger is based upon something that happened in the past, so when you're experiencing anger, you're not present. I'm not suggesting that anger is bad or to be avoided – anger is one of many natural emotions – but I'm suggesting that anger takes you out of the present. Anger can also be a great teacher, but only once we're willing to leave the anger (based upon something in the past) behind in order to move into the present for the learning. Yes, it's important to share with others the impact of their behaviors on us, including the triggering of our anger, but sharing with others from a place of anger rarely serves the communication or the relationship. Rather, it's only when we get back to the present and focus on why we were triggered to anger by a person or situation that we can effectively address the purported cause of our anger. We learn in the present (more on this in a moment), so if you're instead angry in this moment then you're missing the possible learning because of the anger.

This brings us to learning, which happens in the present, but you may be wondering how can I learn from the past without falling into the trap of being in the past (and therefore not present). The answer is simple – we only learn in the present by bringing the past into the present solely for the purpose of the learning. Let's say you had a disagreement with your partner last night and you want to learn from it (e.g. what triggered it, ways to avoid it in the future, different ways to navigate through it, etc.). If you simply think about what happened and get stuck in your feelings of anger, resentment, regret, disappointment, fear, etc., then you're time traveling and not present. However, if you bring the situation into the present for the purpose of learning from it, then you're operating in the present to learn, and learning only happens in the present. We also know from past experiences that interacting and communicating from a place of anger usually limits or precludes our desired outcomes regarding learning, understanding, communicating and relating.

We think we learn, grow and improve in the future, but it's not true – all of these things happen in the present, and the overall improvements get seen and experienced in the future. Think about this situation – you want to get better at public speaking. You're committed, and you invest a great deal of time learning and practicing, and a year from now you say that you've gotten better at public speaking. It's now the future as opposed to when you made the statement and commitment, but all of the improvement happened in the present, moment by moment, when you were learning and practicing. The reality is that all growth happens in the moment – certainly not in the past and never in the future. This present moment is all that we have, and it's to be cherished as the only place where change, growth and connections happen – if we can stay present in it.

Another trap of the non-present is the idea that thinking about things is the same as learning but this is a big lie, one we've culturally embraced to our extreme detriment. Yes, thoughts have value, and we need to think about things, but too often our thinking isn't in the present. I may have just lost you, but let me explain. We think in the present, but those thoughts may not be of the present. If you're thinking about what happened in the past or what you need to do in the future, then you're probably not present. Whether you're present or not depends on what you're thinking about. This may seem confusing, but you'll find it's pretty easy to differentiate which thoughts or thinking processes are present and which are not.

For example, if you're thinking about your upcoming vacation and working on the flight arrangements, then you're present even though you're thinking about something in the future. However, note that what you're actually thinking about is the flight arrangements, which are hap-pening in the present moment. In contrast, if you're worrying about the flight arrangements, thinking that you need to make them soon (rather than actually making them) or worrying about the cost of the flights, then you're not present. This is where it can get a little tricky – are you in the present and making decisions about something or are you not present because you're worrying in some way about something?

Let's look at a simple example in order to understand what's in the present and what's not. You decide to go to the grocery store tomorrow, and here are various possible elements of that process:

Thinking over and over that you need to go to the grocery store tomorrow [Not Present]

Putting a reminder on your calendar to go to the grocery store tomorrow [Present]

Making the grocery list [Present]

Thinking about whether you left anything off the grocery list when you're doing other things [Not Present]

Stressing about whether you have time to go to the grocery store tomorrow [Not Present]

Thinking about how expensive groceries are or about how your partner doesn't help with the groceries [Not Present]

Thinking about the grocery list when you're driving home without writing down the items [likely not present because you'll have to re-create the same thoughts when you're ready to make the list]

The act of grocery shopping if you're solely focused on what you want to buy [Present], but not present if you're thinking about what you have to do at work next week [which explains many of the times we forget something at the store because we're thinking about something else]

From reading the foregoing, you may start to think that being present is complicated, but this example actually highlights the simplicity and sharpness of the present. You're either present or not, and you only act and can be your most productive in the present. The same is true with learning – we learn in the present by bringing the past into the present, not by dwelling on or recycling the past.

You're either present or not, and you only act and can be your most productive in the present.

Now let's look at the ways that time traveling into the future keeps us from the gifts of presence. Fear, anxiety and stress are all based upon time traveling into the future. We feel and experience them in the present, but they're based upon the future. All of these are feelings or experiences we have (rarely helpful and often harmful) because we're thinking and worrying about what has not happened yet (and may never happen!). Here are some common examples of thoughts that keep us from being present:

Just Be Present

I don't know if I'll have enough time to get everything done today.

I'm worried that I won't do well in my meeting tomorrow.

I'm stressed out about my parents coming to visit this weekend.

I can assure you, and you likely will not dispute, that all of these feelings and experiences keep you from being present with whatever or whomever is front of you today. Certainly, these time traveling thoughts keep you from being your best and experiencing your best in this present moment.

Make no mistake – it's important to pay attention to what you have good reason to believe is in your future and to take different actions today (in the present) to prepare for these things. However, if you attempt to take the actions in the present while thinking about the uncertainties of the future, your actions may be less impactful than expected, and your present experience will be diminished – tainted by your fears and anxieties about the future.

But what about nice thoughts about the future? Does the present win over the future thoughts? I say yes, and the reason is that pondering about good things in the future will diminish your present moment and will certainly keep you from being present with the people you're with. As I explained above, whether you're in the present or time traveling in the future depends on the specific context, as seen in this example:

Someday, I want to travel to Europe. [Not Present – this is a thought of what you hope to do in the future and doesn't move you toward that objective]

I'm looking forward to traveling to Europe next month. [Not Present – you looking forward to the future events takes you away from whatever or whomever is in your present]

Discussing your trip to Europe next month with your partner in terms of what you want to do, see and experience. [Present]

Researching your trip to Europe next month [Present]

Booking your airfare to Europe next month [Present]

Thinking about booking your airfare to Europe next month [Not Present]

Are you with me? Do you see the distinctions that differentiate the present from the non-present? Do you see how one feeds you and one distracts you? Time travel into the future is neither good nor bad, but if it's not in the present then it's likely not serving you.

You may not like it, but present IS or is not. You're either in the present or you're not. You're either present with the person you're with or not, and it will shift quickly (and perhaps often) when you're with them. The same is true when it comes to your work – you're either present (and most productive) or you're not present (and less productive). There are challenges to getting and staying present, but whether or not you're present is simple and clear. Now that you better understand the differences, my hope and desire is that you'll use this awareness to find and claim more presence in every part of your life. The gifts and rewards of presence are deep and profound, and they're all just around the corner – just one step away.

Presence Pillars (The Gifts)

It's long been talked about – gifts that keep on giving – but there's no greater or more impactful gift that *keeps on giving* than the gift of presence. Many of you have likely heard this phrase before – give the gift of presence – but do you really understand it and believe it? Perhaps even more important, the gift of presence has a unique aspect that no other gift provides. Presence is a gift that offers something both to the giver and the receiver. If I give someone else the gift of presence and live my life in the present, I receive a multitude of gifts – not from the other person or from the world at large, but from and through the act of being present. In other words, presence is a two-way street by its very nature, which makes it the greatest gift in this realm of the world.

There's no greater or more impactful gift that *keeps on giving* than the gift of presence.

Just Be Present

Let's now look at the many gifts of presence for the giver and the receiver – what I call the Presence Pillars. Once you know them, you'll want to make presence a part of every moment of your existence – not just because you're giving, but because you're ready to receive these incredible presence gifts for yourself.

Let's start with the most powerful gift element of presence, which is experienced by every person who receives your gift. When you care enough to be present, you send a powerful and empowering message to the other person or people. Even if it's typically unstated, being present for another person tells them that they're the most important person in that moment. More tangibly, the person who receives your full presence *feels* the truth that they're the most important person in that moment. This isn't an overstatement, because the state of presence tells the other person that all that matters in that moment is them. As Thich Nhat Hanh wrote, "When you love someone, you want to offer [them] something that can make [them] happy. According to this practice, the most precious thing that you can offer your beloved in your presence" (*No Mud, No Lotus*, 75). Presence – an amazing gift indeed!

The people who receive your gift of presence may not be able to put words or even conscious thought to this, but the gift is received by them even if they're not aware of what exactly is happening. They'll also know that the gift you're giving them is unusual in today's culture. This also makes you unique in being one of the few people capable and committed enough to give this gift of presence.

Unfortunately, the opposite is also true – when you fail to be present, the message communicated to the other person is that someone else or something else, even if just a thought, is more important than them. You may not like this, but that doesn't change its reality. While this may be the most typical scenario today, that doesn't excuse it nor does it change its outcome and impact. The simplicity of presence is this – if you give the gift of presence, that person receives and experiences the gift of being the most important person in the room in that moment. If, however, you fail to deliver the gift of presence, then the person receives the message (even if unconsciously) that something or someone else is more important than them in that moment.

Some of you may think that presence doesn't matter in interpersonal interactions or that people can't tell if you're present, but presence deeply matters and people know whether someone is fully present with them or not. Sometimes it's crazy obvious and someone calls you on it (i.e. "Where are you right now?"), or perhaps it's subtler, but they can sense you're not fully there based upon their experience of you. They either experience presence or not. They experience feeling like the most important person or they experience feeling like they're one of many priorities in that moment – if they're a priority at all. The most empowering element of this gift is that you get to decide which message you'll deliver. Will you give this gift of presence to others, or will you withhold it?

Another incredible and mutually shared gift of presence relates to the reality that presence requires vulnerability. Because vulnerability is a foundational element of giving and receiving presence, the natural corollary is that giving and receiving presence is a critical element of demonstrating, modeling and building trust. Think about it – are you likely to give your full presence to someone that you don't trust? Are you likely to receive the gift of presence from someone that you don't trust or who doesn't trust you?

Here's where it gets interesting. Because presence requires vulnerability, and because many of you are unwilling to trust early, this makes giving the gift of presence to someone that you don't fully trust highly vulnerable. However, giving someone the gift of presence actually allows you to build trust with that person. Your act of trusting enough to give presence communicates a message in action and energy that will help to build and accelerate your trust levels with the other person.

Perhaps, the question when it comes to presence and trust isn't whether you're ready, but whether you're willing. Whatever your answer, just know this – your gift of presence to others will pay huge and immediate dividends to yourself and your relationships in terms of building, growing and accelerating trust. It's just the truth of the gift of presence.

Another important message that's communicated through the gift of presence is the profound message of unconditional love. I'm guessing that you didn't see that message or perspective coming, but it's true. When you're willing to be fully present with another person, you're offering them the gift of unconditional love. Think about it – how can you be fully present for another person while you're judging them? The answer is clear – you can't do both. You can't judge another person and be fully present for them. In fact, the act and energy of judgment will take you out of presence. You have to remember that being present is so much more than simply listening – even actively listening. Presence requires that we're here with them, listening to them, hearing them, witnessing them

The question when it comes to presence and trust isn't whether you're ready, but whether you're willing.

– and judgment is inconsistent with all of these. The act of delivering an unconditional love experience requires the gift of presence.

Now we come to the holy grails of presence – those gifts that you receive when and to the extent that you're capable of being fully present in your life. First, let me be clear that you're unlikely to always be present (24 / 7). While I consider myself to be often and extensively present, I have moments when the other slips in and my presence slips away. I can feel it and sense it, and I know when I'm not present because the gifts of presence – the holy grails – are missing. The question isn't whether you're present all the time, but whether you're able to find presence and recreate it more and more every day. Like life, the road to presence is also a journey.

Here are what I consider the holy grails of presence, all of which form the foundation not only of this chapter, but of this entire book because these grails all lead you and me to the ultimate gift of being unstoppable. When you're present, you're:

Stressless – Stress can't co-exist with presence.

Fearless – Fear exists only outside of presence.

Regretless – If you're having regrets about the past, then you're no longer present.

Shameless – Shame comes from thoughts we have that we're less than / not enough, and those don't exist in the present. When you're present, you're worthy and more than enough.

Joyful – Joy is one of the key gifts of presence.

Peaceful – Presence is the source of peace since it can't co-exist with chaos and uncertainty.

How's that for a core list of gifts of presence? Together, they form the foundation that leads you to being unshakeable and unstoppable.

You may have heard the question, "What would you do if you knew you couldn't fail?" While presence doesn't guarantee success, it does create the optimum mindset and energy for achieving whatever objectives you desire. Imagine if you weren't feeling the fear, you weren't regretting your past, you were trusting that you're worthy and enough, and you had no stress or uncertainty. These are the foundational elements for what it means to experience being unshakeable and unstoppable. Thus, this book's journey has taken you from your current state to the state of unstoppable – the journey to your unstoppable you!

Be Present Now

Now it's up to you. You have the presence awareness and the presence tools, and you also have the clarity about the gifts you give and receive when you're willing to be present. Presence is calling you, calling all of us. The present is waiting for you. Most important, all of your goals, desires and objectives are waiting for you, and they're waiting just on the other side of presence – full presence –Just One Step away! You may not have realized that you were so close, but now you see it. Now you know it and feel it. The only question is whether you'll trust it – and trust yourself – enough to take the leap into the present. Now is the time, and the only question is up to you – will you leap, will you trust, will you commit and will you claim the present for yourself and everyone around you in your life and leadership?

All of your goals, desires and objectives are waiting for you, and they're waiting just on the other side of presence - full presence –Just One Step away!

Chapter 16

Just Follow

*Y*ou're nearly at the end of this journey of awakening, discovery and awareness, and while your personal journey will continue long past your reading of this book, it's important to allow your journey through *Just One Step* to end. While I've shared many concepts, ideas, perspectives and tools in this book, my hope is that you've experienced them in the way I intended – simple to follow, even if challenging to fully implement. I also want to give you a short overview of a life map to follow as you continue your walk through life and as you make all of the ideas in this book part of your daily journey. What follows is what I call a *Life Formula* – because you can use it to navigate your life differently from this day forward, one step at a time. But you must be willing to follow.

This life formula came to me in a conversation with a friend that I hadn't seen for many years. She'd moved out of town years before but had recently moved back to the Cleveland area. We were catching up, and I was sharing the state of my life and my experiences with her – lots of joy and fun, travels and adventure, little or no stress, and differently navigating the challenging parts of life including loss and grief. She expressed the differences she was seeing in me, and at one point she asked me what my "secret" was to creating this life experience. I started to say that there's no secret, but then the following came out of me with the greatest certainty and clarity. While I'd shared many points relating to this before, I shared it with her for the first time in a sort of formula – what I now call the 5 x 4 for life.

Five simple concepts for living an enriched life—each one only four words. While they may not always be easy to achieve, I've found them to be true, and their simplicity has allowed me to live life differently than ever before and differently than most people do. My hope is that with every passing day more of you embrace this 5 x 4 formula and achieve more of what you've been desiring in your businesses, careers, relationships and lives. And of course, just one step at a time!

Here's the 5 x 4 formula for life:

1. I Only Control Me
2. I Am Here Now
3. Detach from the Outcomes
4. It Will Be Okay
5. Just Take a Breath

It may seem too good to be true, but make no mistake about it – these five concepts are significant shifts for most of us, but they're simple. Perhaps they're *so good that they're true*. Now, let's take a closer look at these elements of the 5 x 4 life formula.

I Only Control Me

It's simple and absolutely true. You don't control anyone else or anything else. We all know this, and many of you acknowledge this, but you don't live your life as if it's true. All or nearly all of your stress comes from or relates to things that you don't control, and embracing this truth is one pivotal foundation for a life shift.

Our biggest problem with this part of the formula is that we're highly resistant to the idea that we don't control things beyond ourselves. In fact, we're downright arrogant about it, and I've had the most interesting discussions over the past years as people have tried to convince me about how they control things outside themselves. We don't, and you don't!

Yes, we have the ability to influence things and people, but we don't control them, and acknowledging this truth – and living in accordance with it – is at the heart of an amazing life experience. Once you admit that you only control yourself, then and only then do you know when and where to direct all of your awareness, attention and action.

> Once you admit that you only control yourself, then and only then do you know when and where to direct all of your awareness, attention and action.

I Am Here Now

The next foundation for life is committing to and achieving full presence in your life – certainly when interacting with others, but also with everything you do in life. Whether you're taking a walk, working on a project, playing a game, or enjoying a vacation, being fully present will enhance and enrich your experience, the experience of everyone around you and your outcomes.

Chapter 15 above covers this element – presence – in great detail, and it's worth reminding ourselves here and now that without presence the other life formula elements will fall apart. They all work together and rely upon each other, but without presence the whole life formula will come up short in creating your new and enhanced life experience.

Recently, I was teaching a workshop that included affirmations, and a new affirmation for myself popped into my head. It struck me like a lightning bolt, and it's the outcome of both my personal journey and my deep understanding of the power of presence. The affirmation that came to me was simple: I'm here. I'm Here. I'M HERE! Right now, in this moment, I'm allowing my presence to be enough because I'm enough.

Are you ready to claim such an affirmation for yourself? Are you ready to let presence be your mission? Are you ready to allow this present moment to be enough, knowing that you're already enough? This is your journey and your choice to make on the road back to the present.

Detach from the Outcomes

This will be a tough one for many of you because you still arrogantly believe that you control outcomes, just like you falsely believe you control things and people outside of yourself. Detachment involves being fully and passionately committed to your objectives and desires with high expectations, while staying detached from the outcomes. As simple as this sounds, many of you deny it's truth. You may say the right words, but you internally believe that you actually control outcomes. This is your ego talking.

Certainly, you have influence on outcomes by your efforts, mindsets, etc., but you don't control the outcomes. Many of us have been told to be realistic or to lower our expectations so we're not disappointed, but that sets us up for lesser outcomes. However, when you're able to set and commit to high expectations, while detaching from the outcomes, you'll achieve a level of peacefulness and impact beyond your current imagination.

The question isn't whether you *can* detach from the outcomes, but whether you're *willing* to detach from them. Attachment to outcomes is a choice – your choice – and you can likewise choose to detach from them. You may want to resist this element, but it's essential to transforming your life's experience, journey and outcomes. In this magic formula, detaching from the outcomes will actually enhance your outcomes, right from the beginning.

Are you willing to admit that you don't control everything so that you can have more of what you want in your life, career, business and relationships? Well, are you?

It Will Be Okay (It's Already Okay)

When you consider this entire formula, this might be the most difficult part of all. Admittedly, this is the only one that I can't say is a clear truth. The reason is that this foundation is based upon trust and faith. Whether you have a faith practice (religious, spiritual or otherwise) or not, this element is critical to achieving the overall objectives and shifts because without it you'll fall victim to many of your current realities of stress, uncertainty and doubt. No matter what happens in my life or around me today and no matter what outcomes are achieved or not achieved, I deeply trust that everything will be fine – including me. I can't prove that this is true, but I'm living this powerful maxim and experiencing its truth.

In fact, since I shared this formula for the first time (two years ago), my perspective on this element has shifted. I no longer believe and live that everything will be okay – my truth (and hopefully your truth) is that *everything is already okay.* What, you say? How can everything already be okay? Because it already is – everything is already okay, and that includes you, but only if you're willing to believe it and trust it.

This doesn't mean you don't have to take action or that you can sit around, do nothing and hope that things will be okay. This formula element is about trusting that everything is already okay and taking action in that direction at the same time. It's a paradox, and embracing paradox is essential to making the shifts I've offered you in this book. If it sounds crazy, you're right – it is crazy, if you think it's crazy. However, imagine how your life will be different every day if you know and trust that everything, including you, is already okay – before the day even begins. What impact would this way of living have on your levels of stress, on your relationships and on your life achievements?

But here's the hitch – this element doesn't ensure that things will always turn out the way you planned or hoped, just that everything will be okay … *in fact, it already is, and so are you!*

Just Take a Breath

For you doubters of things that seem too simple, this will be a difficult foundation to embrace. You might say or think, "How can taking a breath change everything?" but that's the real truth – taking a breath does change everything. My friend and fellow coach Jim Smith has been sharing this wisdom and truth with leaders for many years – the power and impact of breathing – and it's so simple that its power often gets ignored or underestimated. I often invite people to take a breath, particularly when they're feeling stress or uncertainty, and they almost always say, "I'm already breathing." My response is that they're survival breathing, but taking a real, deep breath (or two or three) will help them relax, get present and dump all or most of whatever stress they're experiencing. The magic of the breath is profound, simple and real – catch yourself not breathing, and take a breath.

As I shared in Chapter 15, taking an intentional breath not only brings you to the present, but it requires that you get present in order to take the purposeful breath. Thus, the intentional breath and presence work together and support each other. The great thing about the simplicity of the breath is that it doesn't involve any risk. There's no downside to taking a purposeful breath – only upside. If you're worried about what people might think if they see you taking a deep breath, then the only question is what matters more to you – what people think of you breathing or you enhancing your presence, reducing your stress and accelerating your relationships. Not a bad trade-off for just a few simple breaths.

There it is – the 5 x 4 formula for a peaceful, connected and impactful life. In answer to the question I know many of you are asking right now, yes, it IS just that simple. I know it works because it's the way I've been living for the past two years. Admittedly, I have occasions when I forget or lose track of this life formula, but it's the core of my life experience today, and it's deepening every day. The deaths of my mom and uncle, as well as various personal, business and relationship challenges, have tested and proven to me the truth and impact of the 5 x 4 life formula in all of life's situations.

I'm grateful to have found and clarified this different way of living and leading, and I'm offering it to each one of you to help you shift the way you navigate and experience every aspect of your lives. These are the foundations that I share with my coaching clients and support them in achieving. These are also the foundations that are at the core of the personal retreats I lead (Arrows of Truth).

The question isn't whether the 5 x 4 life formula works, but whether you're willing to let go of control, put aside your ego, and allow yourself to trust enough to receive what you desire. If you're ready to shift your life experience, the 5 x 4 is your solution. And like everything in this book, every element of the 5 x 4 life formula happens in simple steps – *always just one step at a time.*

The Journey Continues

As we conclude our journey together – the journey back to the present – I leave you with this truth. The issue isn't whether what I've shared in this book will create the outcomes I've described – the question is whether you'll be willing to let go of your old ways of thinking and living, willing to let go of your false sense of control and willing to let go of your arrogance in believing that life and success is about making things happen (rather than facilitating things to happen). It's your choice. Are you willing to open yourself up to something new – new ways of thinking, perceiving, believing and acting – in order to have new experiences in every nook and corner of your life?

Unless your life and leadership are fully and authentically everything you desire, why not try on something new? Take new and different steps in the direction of what your heart desires and be willing not to know all the answers. Be willing to take more risks, including emotional risks. Be willing to know less and trust more. Be willing to think less and allow more. The road of your life is still being created at your feet every day. It's not my road or anyone else's road – it's your road and you're the co-creator of the road in front of you with every step.

> The road of your life is still being created at your feet every day. It's not my road or anyone else's road – it's your road and you're the co-creator of the road in front of you with every step.

I knew that my journey to the Camino de Santiago would be a profound experience, but I never knew the depth to which the journey would inform me, fill me and transform me. Certainly, I couldn't have imagined the many lessons that the Camino fed into me – lessons which I've shared with all of you in this book. As I said at the beginning, you don't need to take your own Camino journey in order to reap the benefits and rewards of a life led and lived in accordance with the principles I've shared in *Just One Step*. Indeed, it's not about the Camino at all, but the Camino provided the context for these lessons. Whether or not you ever take a single step on the Camino de Santiago in Spain, you now have what you need to take your own steps on the journey to a different way of living and leading – that is, if you're ready to create more influence and impact; if you're ready to enhance your relationships; if you're ready to be the leader you've always wanted to be; if you're ready to live life with less stress and more joy.

I woke up in a hotel in Raleigh, NC, which led me to a pilgrimage in Spain, and that pilgrimage led me back to the essence of life and the essence of me. This book is the outcome of discovering the best of me and of life, and I share that journey and its lessons with you. I never knew that the Camino journey would inform and transform my life experience and life journey forever, and the transformation in me has been profound. My deep wish and blessing is that my sharing of this journey will do the same for you – that you'll find your way to always living and being unstoppable. Always remember, the journey to your unstoppable you begins and ends with *Just One Step.*

About the Author

Beginning as a successful lawyer, Jeff Nischwitz first modeled courageous change when he left the corporate law firm where he was a partner to take the leap into entrepreneurship by creating his own law firm. After building and growing that firm into a northeast Ohio success story, Jeff did what few dare to even consider: *he left that which he knew and which was successful to go in search of his true calling.* For Jeff, getting by or merely succeeding without loving what he does was not acceptable.

When asked how he transitioned from entrepreneurial lawyer to international speaker and transformation coach, Jeff is known to say something like the following:

> "I'd love to tell you that it was a great plan, brilliantly executed, but it's more like a car wreck where the car rolled over several times and somehow landed on its wheels. I was injured and even had some broken bones, but I was alive and the car was still drivable. So I took off in the direction it was pointing and I've been going ever since."

Jeff is a man who has walked his own journey from "nice guy" to good man and from "successful" business owner to inspirational speaker and personal transformation coach. He's a man who has had and continues to have various challenges, setbacks and failures, yet continues to stand back up, dust himself off, arm himself with the lessons learned, and leap back into life.

Emerson posited that "life is a journey, not a destination," and Jeff Nischwitz has indeed been on a journey, the journey of a lifetime. Jeff's most recent life journey on the road to Santiago de Compostela in northern Spain – *the Camino de Santiago* – is the foundation of this book.

Facilitator of Truth ... Accelerator ... Relationship Builder ... Master Storyteller ... Chief Inquisitor ... Story Debunker ... Disruptor ... Transformational Coach ... Inspirational Model for Change! This is how business leaders and clients describe Jeff Nischwitz. Jeff is the Founder and Chief Snow Globe Shaker of The Nischwitz Group, a speaking, consulting and coaching company that transforms people and organizations—*one truth at a time*! With people and relationships, perception IS the only reality and the moment that we shift our perceptions, we immediately shift our experience. *Just One Step* offers you many different shifts and truths that will fundamentally transform every nook and cranny of your life.

Big in stature and bigger in heart, Jeff Nischwitz is a force of nature and is shaking up leaders and lives across the country and the globe with his messages about conscious leadership, self-awareness and impact focus, and his courageous injection of authenticity, vulnerability and intimate relationships into the world. As an international keynote speaker and master facilitator, Jeff energizes audiences and challenges people to shake things up in their leadership, businesses and lives. Jeff's audiences experience disruptive thinking, challenging questions, vulnerable sharing, and inspired perspectives on the path to achieving more impact and influence through and throughout life—an experience that's been called "Getting Jeffed!"

Jeff is also the author of three other books:

- *Think Again! Innovative Approaches to the Business of Law* (American Bar Association 2007), which offers creative and practical advice on building an exceptional law firm.
- *Unmask: Let Go of Who You're "Supposed" to Be & Unleash Your True Leader* (Motivational Press 2014), a road map for navigating your own personal journey as a leader in your business, career, relationships and life.

- *Arrows of Truth: Simple Shifts for Personal Transformation* (Eagle Heart Press 2016), a workbook style practical guide for creating real change in your life, relationships and leadership.

Known professionally for his challenging questions and unique perspectives, and personally for his love of his two sons, playing baseball, his travel adventures and his annual history trips with his Dad, Jeff Nischwitz now says "come with me" and brings you along on his Camino adventure in Spain through *Just One Step*.

To contact Jeff Nischwitz, visit www.nischwitzgroup.com.